ACE TEAMS

To Carol and Gillian with our love

ACE TEAMS

Creating star performance in business

Andrew Leigh and
Michael Maynard

Butterwoth-Heinemann Ltd
Linacre House, Jordan Hill, Oxford OX2 8DP

℟ A member of the Reed Elsevier group

OXFORD LONDON BOSTON
MUNICH NEW DELHI SINGAPORE SYDNEY
TOKYO TORONTO WELLINGTON

First published 1993
First published as a paperback edition 1994

British Library Cataloguing in Publication Data
Leigh, Andrew
    ACE Teams: Creating star performance in
    business
I. Title.   II. Maynard, Michael
    658.4

ISBN 0 7506 1883 3

Photoset by Deltatype Ltd, Ellesmere Port, Cheshire
Printed and bound in Great Britain by Clays Ltd, St Ives plc

CONTENTS

PREVIEW

You've bought your ticket – the price of this book! – and are settled in your seat. Now the lights begin to dim. Around you the noise dies down; any moment the curtain will rise, and you sit there perhaps wondering what this show is all about.

Simply, it's about building superb business teams – quickly – using tried and tested practices from the performing arts.

Meanwhile, here's a quick preview of what you're in for. Certainly not your average management or business book, we hope. We've ploughed through too many of them ourselves to inflict another on you.

Instead we want you to have fun with ACE teams, and since we've loved producing the show, why shouldn't the audience enjoy it too? We hope to surprise you, so won't give too much away now. But here are just a few points you may find will make the experience even better.

First, after an introductory Curtain raiser, the book falls into three sections or acts, each with its own prologue. Common to most theatrical productions, there are several scenes within each act. This is the main body of the book and covers the thrust of our argument and ideas on team development.

Second, if you're as busy as we think you are, you'd probably like a quick summary of each chapter – or in the case of ACE teams the various scenes of the three acts. Each scene is summarized by a visual story board at the end of each scene. So if you really can't sit through the whole show, a glance at the story boards tells you our basic messages.

Finally, right at the end of the book (pp. 209–218), you'll find yet another form of summary, this one based on an idea we borrowed from the BP culture change programme. Here the various scenes are condensed on a single page into more conventional business and management language. No time for any more, the curtain is at last rising . . .

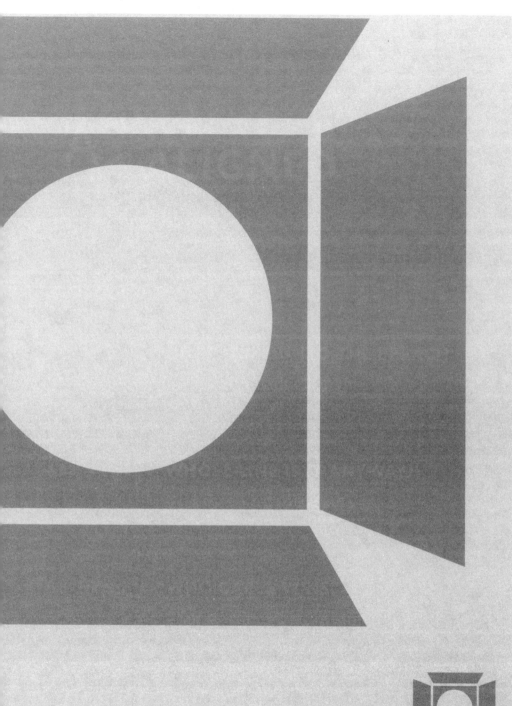

CURTAIN RAISER

CURTAIN RAISER

We overhear a chance meeting between two directors. One is a managing director of a business, the other is a theatre director:

MANAGING DIRECTOR:	*It's you! This is really lucky, you're just the person I wanted to see.*
THEATRE DIRECTOR:	*What's up?*
MANAGING DIRECTOR:	*I want to talk to you about teams.*
THEATRE DIRECTOR:	*You're going to tell me again what a great team you've got, aren't you?*
MANAGING DIRECTOR:	*Well, it's true I've built a fine team around me. It's taken me two years hard labour.*
THEATRE DIRECTOR:	*And they're performing well?*
MANAGING DIRECTOR:	*They certainly have been.*
THEATRE DIRECTOR:	*Looks like I could learn something from your experience.*
MANAGING DIRECTOR:	*You probably could, though this time I'd like to pick YOUR brains. You see the situation is changing, and changing fast.*
THEATRE DIRECTOR:	*I can identify with that. The performing arts are always in a constant state of flux. I used to think 'stability' was a type of marker pen!*
MANAGING DIRECTOR:	*Perfect. I knew you'd be the person to help. I've got to create an entirely new team. But this one has to be exceptional, one that performs absolutely at its best. And I don't have the luxury of much development time.*
THEATRE DIRECTOR:	*You mean you've got to build a team instantly – and it's got to perform brilliantly?*
MANAGING DIRECTOR:	*You see my problem. I want a really ace team, and fast. What would YOU do?*

Why can actors, in a mere 3 weeks, make a high quality product? Or how does an orchestra, with only days of rehearsal, produce outstanding results? And what explains the power of a newly formed dance group to create a masterpiece in weeks rather than months or years?

We've always been fascinated with these questions. Our work in business is about getting people to work together more creatively and effectively. It has become a crusade with us; for example, we regularly run lunchtime seminars, bringing people from the field of human resource development round a table to explore these issues. They come from all sorts of organizations to exchange their experiences of good and bad teams. Both we and they learn a great deal from each other.

On Tuesday 3 March 1992, at a few minutes past 8 pm after a pre-interval performance of Beethoven's Pastoral Symphony that was an incoherent mess, conductor Franz Welser-Möst walked on to the podium in a Japanese concert hall and ignored the applause. He tore into Beethoven's Fifth Symphony with demonic force. The terrifying performance took every corner on two wheels, the risks were enormous, yet from first to last bar the structure was in place. The individuality was unmistakable. It was a stunning new interpretation that took no prisoners, admitted no weaknesses. After endless recalls, a member of the orchestra finally whispered: 'Franz, something happened tonight'.

We also constantly explore the issues with our clients, and have studied companies that have made radical culture shifts in their organizations through a commitment to teamwork. Our own commitment to teamwork produced our company, and indeed this book. Like you, we want to know what works in team-building and what's new.

Our own experience has proved a useful source of ideas. One of us was a senior manager for many years, trying to get the best from teams. The other was a professional actor for nearly 20 years, working in several hundred different creative teams. Together we think we know quite a lot about teams. Yet two pressing questions have surfaced, questions that explain the reasons for the rest of the book:

- How can you produce exceptional teams, quickly?
- With their enormous experience of building outstanding teams quickly, what lessons can the performing arts offer business?

But, first, why does it matter? What's driving many business organizations to rethink team-building in the first place?

Diversity

We are seeing increasing diversity in the types of organization in our midst. In turn, they trigger a growing variety in the sorts of teams being created. Take, for example, pulsating organizations – ones that grow and shrink to a regular rhythm.

These companies may gear up for an annual model change, or, like seasonal businesses, treble their staff at certain times of the year, then force a similar reduction until the next cycle. Such organizations not only have unique information and communication requirements, they also need new ways to create, stimulate and eventually dismantle their teams. Then do it all over again some time later.

Alternatively, take the mega consortia, where massive combinations of resources, drawn from an immense range of different enterprises, are temporarily welded together. Think of the Channel Tunnel, the development in the Isle of Dogs, the creation of EuroDisney. All demand the rapid formation of effective, multi-disciplinary teams expected to be up and running in maybe months.

The professions too are undergoing major shifts, faced with increasing competition often enforced by changes in legislation. New arrangements are transforming somewhat feudal systems into more customer-responsive teams. Accountants, once cushioned by cosy audit contracts, are having to create more proactive audit teams that think and act differently to their predecessors.

Solicitors in Britain are having to learn about marketing and how to create instant teams to pitch for new business. Architects, facing a hard time in a recessionary climate, are also having to consider whether their old team habits are the best.

Networking has also taken root in many organizations as a way of working and getting things done. This provokes entirely new sorts of informal, loosely linked teams, which may have revolving leadership and constantly altering membership.

Decentralization and a war of attrition on bureaucracy and middle managers are placing additional demands on the remaining executives to use their human resources more creatively. Not only must they exercise new skills, such as how to stimulate and develop their own staff, they must learn new, less authoritarian ways of team management.

As companies redesign themselves and as ever richer patterns of human arrangements emerge, our concept of teamwork is changing. It's no longer always so clear what a team is, who leads it or even when it started. Neatly packaged roles and titles look increasingly irrelevant in the face of demands for initiative, inventiveness, creativity, and even fun and enjoyment.

Flatter hierarchies, profit centres, and demands for total quality are putting more power in the hands of front-line staff. Contracting out to smaller companies and a dozen other trends are force-feeding the emergence of different and often extremely temporary teams. These are increasingly expected to be better than just average. As part of this process of rising expectations, star performing teams are no longer regarded as the exception.

Motorola Inc. is just one example of companies with rising expectations that their teams should be exceptional, i.e. star performers.

In June 1986 Motorola gave a newly formed 24-member team a tough challenge – design a new radio pager and a world class computer facility to control all aspects of its production. The facility had to be able to produce each pager with a 99.9997 per cent probability that each one would be perfect. The team was given 18 months to do it.

They met the challenge. The new plant was created in Florida and worked as required, with 17 days to spare.

Given these developments, what can we say about teams that retains its relevance in the midst of such an onslaught of changing demands and evolving patterns of human behaviour? Certainly the traditional models of teams and team-building are beginning to look threadbare, and maladapted to modern business needs.

Underlying these changes in how teams are being viewed is the requirement for quick results. Once team-building could be a leisurely affair, spread over months, even years. Now the sheer speed of change in many market sectors makes long lead times unacceptable. People want star performance – NOW.

We've called the emerging new requirement a demand for ACE teams, because they are expected to be star performers in their field. Their members are no longer strictly interchangeable with anyone else in the company or someone who could be hired from outside. Instead people in today's and tomorrow's teams increasingly consist of skilled knowledge workers using their brains rather than brawn.

Remove any one of this new type of team member and the whole group may cease to function effectively. Such teams often operate in a knowledge-intensive, information-based world, where managers struggle to create groups capable of tackling the challenges and opportunities facing their fast-moving enterprises.

Pressure for instant and improved teams has prompted people to search some unusual territory – everything from rigging a ship or climing mountains to playing in a football team or plunging down potholes. Yet more than many other team pursuits, the performing arts, whether theatre, music, opera, dance or even film, are more integrated with the fabric of our culture and our experience. They are familiar and much of their team activity contains directly transferable skills and know-how.

In 1990 we took our own research a stage further, in order to distil some of these performing arts ideas. We brought together a group of actors, theatre directors and business consultants, who met regularly over several months, to unravel the mystery of what the performing arts could offer the average business. In particular we wanted to clarify the factors permitting the creative and performing arts to consistently and rapidly achieve outstanding team performance.

To solve the mystery, the group systematically explored what the performing arts do well in a team setting and why. Wherever they looked in the arts, they detected common sets of behaviour or operating rules. Their consultant colleagues suggested these were equally relevant in business and industry.

As we've seen earlier, business organizations face a challenge that the performing arts constantly tackle: rapidly creating a team, with each member having different skills or training, and then asking it to produce high quality results fast. The group began to identify specific tasks the performing arts do well, usually even better than business or industry.

The first of these was demonstrated by a challenging scenario:

Imagine you are a senior executive in a company, with a tight deadline to design and develop a new product. You will personally launch it to an audience of 1,000 of your customers. They await it with interest and have high expectations.

If they like it, they will acclaim your considerable achievement. You will personally receive their appreciation in the most potent way possible. They will cheer and applaud your efforts. Briefly you will experience the gratitude of those who admire you and your work. You will be proud of yourself and your product.

On the other hand, should the product displease your customers, an opposite and equally strong reaction occurs. You will still be in the limelight. But this time you will experience repeated waves of rejection and hostility.

As the senior manager, you are personally responsible for the failure of the product. You may not offer any excuses or justifications, such as lack of time, poor supplies, lack of funds, or inadequate staff. Instead of acclamation you will experience public humiliation on a grand scale. It will hurt. However, you also know that you have another group of 1,000 customers arriving next day and the next. Again you will face them personally with your product.

Intensity of experience

That is how it is for the performer. In exploring what makes an ACE team, we realized early on that a powerful reason is *the intensity of a performer's own experience*.

Stories of audiences stoning performers are rare, but even if they merely boo, the experience is still hideous. Comedians rightly talk about 'dying on stage'. The humiliation is as close as you can get to a near-death experience. Performers take these risks in a determined way. In the best companies they support each other to the highest level, and their commitment to quality is supreme.

The high-risk nature of the 'front-stage' experience stimulates special ways of working 'back-stage', in rehearsal. Professor Iain Mangham of the School of Management, University of Bath, has also researched performing arts teams and has identified the *non-stop search for excellence*.

No self-respecting performing arts team plans a mediocre production of *Hamlet*, or launches a Beethoven Symphony with the attitude of 'let's just get it over and done with'. Rather the reverse. It strives to be outstanding and produce a masterpiece.

Members of such teams also take personal responsibility. Their deep commitment to the product and respect for their paying customers ensure their sense of ownership is high.

Later we shall show how business and industry can provide more emphasis on taking personal responsibility. Personal pride in the product and willingness to take responsibility exist in all successful companies.

The excellence trip

" Either dance well or leave the ballroom. "

Greek proverb

Excellence has enjoyed a higher profile in the business world with the undoubted impact of the bestseller on this subject, *In Search of Excellence*, by Peters and Waterman. Yet many companies found it difficult to translate the lessons from this compendium of success stories. What worked in Hewlett Packard was not always applicable at home.

The excellence trip spawned droves of failed customer-care schemes, countless total-quality quagmires and a mass of seldom-reported disasters of trying to influence company culture. A senior National Westminster executive once confessed to us that the bank had invested a king's ransom in trying to alter the company culture, and 3 years later nothing much had really changed.

If genuine excellence is to prevail it usually demands that you do something radically different, not more of the same. What would be different in many companies would be a conscious, lasting effort to:

- Build commitment.
- Generate excitement.
- Be creative.
- Use each person's unique talent.
- Develop trust.
- Unlock personal energy.

Commitment

" I don't think you should ever manage anything that you don't care passionately about. "

D. Coleman, Vice President and CFO, Apple Computer Corporation

Few artistic endeavours succeed without a strong commitment. It must come from within, not be imposed from outside by a ruthless management. When people are committed, they give all of themselves at work, and show it. They make suggestions, attend to detail, enjoy their role, are willing to try something new, have pride in their work and abilities, develop their talents and skills, make every minute at work useful, get it right first time, co-operate, are trustworthy, constantly seek improvements, show loyalty, make that extra effort and acknowledge each other's contribution.

Without these signs of commitment no artistic performance of any quality would succeed. No successful business team will manage without these types of behaviour either. However, the performing arts have long taken it for granted that building such commitment is perfectly normal. It is not exceptional. Because it is unexceptional, business can learn from what has become routine elsewhere.

We shall examine later how such commitment is generated. What is important now is the recognition that there is no real difference between the process of building commitment within a performing group of actors and a performing group of managers. The same principles that work within the peforming arts succeed equally in business.

Generating excitement

IBM once hired a massive sports stadium, packing it with employees, and the family and friends of employees. As each IBM salesman came running into the stadium, his respective sales figures were flashed onto the giant electronic scoreboard to the resounding applause of the audience. No one who took part could deny the excitement of the occasion.

Another recent and even more public example would be Rumbelow's Employee of the Year presenting the cup to the winning team at the 1991 League Cup Final at Wembley. Whatever difficulties the company later faced, at the time its commitment to success in such a high profile way created a great stir. To see an ordinary employee performing a task that we so often associate with Royalty made a significant impact with staff and managers alike.

Successful teams, whether in the performing arts or in business, generate excitement. The performing arts, though, have uncovered many of the keys to creating excitement, causing people to commit themselves deeply and be stimulated about achieving team results. Again it is a matter of everyday work practice.

The way excitement is fostered in the performing arts is relatively inexpensive compared to the solutions adopted by many businesses. The incentive travel business, for example, now spends a staggering £10 billion world-wide to send employees on expensive and adventurous trips abroad.

When one talks with business managers about their responsibility to create excitement, there is perhaps a grudging admission that this may need to happen for sales staff. Yet the task is seldom seen as central to the leadership role. We are also struck in our work with organizations of all kinds at the low levels of acknowledgement, appreciation and celebration.

Again, we'll explore later how to create excitement within the team. At this stage it is merely important to mark its key role in the performing arts and its still minor place in the behaviour and practice of most business teams.

Being creative

" **With the revolutionary rise of the new wealth creation system, it is not a fraction of the working population but a substantial and ever expanding number whose productivity depends on precisely the freedom to create everything from new product designs to new computer logics, metaphors, scientific insights and epistemologies.** "

Alvin Toffler, Power Shift

There's hardly any dispute that a team in the performing arts, such as a dance group or group of actors, should be creative. Not so in business. The two words today's managers have most difficulty in confronting are 'power' and 'creativity'.

Power is commonly dismissed as a dirty word, even though to make things happen managers undoubtedly need to act purposefully and powerfully. This does not mean domination or exploitation, but the ability to use one's innate strengths in a way that makes things happen. A Rolls-Royce engine is powerful. So is a senior manager. So is the director of a movie on a film set. The issue is – how is that power used and exercised? Does it fuel the creative endeavour of a team or does it merely keep people in their place?

Creativity in business is frequently relegated to such specialist groups as advertisers, designers or researchers. Successful business teams though are ones that are the most creative, ingenious or inventive in seeking results.

The stereotypes of the two worlds of arts and business are:

Business	Arts
Profit-driven	Passionate
Logical	Crazy
Rational	Irrational
Factual	Intuitive
Introverted	Extroverted
Pragmatic	Flexible
Bureaucratic	Free-spirit
Operational	Dreamers
Systematic	Unpredictable
Sensible	Eccentric
Practical	Creative

You need only observe some of our top entrepreneurs at work and how they have achieved their success, however, to give the lie to stereotypes. To call Richard Branson or Anita Roddick bureaucratic, introverted or uncreative would be foolish.

Equally, when you see how efficient and practical creative artists need to be these days, they can hardly be classed as disorganized vagabonds. Successful teams and their organizations need an essential mix of both sets of qualities, and the stereotypes therefore are outdated. Yet, as with all change, there are the inevitable teething problems.

Creativity as a process is making a slow comeback in business after hitting the headlines in the 1970s. For a while many people went overboard for creativity, with specialists earning a nice living teaching business people how to think and act creatively. But it was creativity without much context, and the inevitable happened. When all the workshops, brainstorming and lateral thinking did not produce the answers to business woes, creativity was discarded as yet another panacea that had gone wrong.

Gradually, though, the central importance of creativity is making a comeback. An increasing number of business leaders openly acknowledge the importance of creativity as the correct response to an environment where rapid change is the norm.

To make sense of creativity within business, one needs to place it in the context of the team. ACE teams learn to use and combine the creativity of the individuals within them. If our research into the unused potential of many people within organizations is correct, there is an enormous reservoir of creative potential ready to serve companies.

Tapping into this potential is already a major concern of such firms as Ford, the Rover Group and Grand Met. These organizations have begun offering employees resources to enable them to learn without necessarily insisting that what they learn is central to the company's immediate needs. The assumption is that unlocking individuals' wishes to steer their own development will cause them to make a more valuable contribution to the company.

In the performing arts, tapping into creative potential is an everyday occurrence and does not merit headlines or admiring articles in business magazines. Those in the performing arts have long since learned that the starting point for a successful team is creativity, and assume that without it there will be no star performance.

It is this combination of creativity and power that is so effective. People using their creative powers get results. Teams using their creative powers get even bigger results. And companies releasing the creative powers of each individual produce outstanding results. Releasing the creative powers of each individual produces results that are 'more than the sum of the parts'.

How to tap into individual and team creativity is something that business can learn to do much better than at present, and the performing arts have much to share, as we shall see later.

Using each person's unique talent

> **" Talent lies in your choice of drama coach. "**
>
> *Stella Adler (Marlon Brando's choice)*

The belief that every person has a unique contribution is another norm within the successful performing arts' team. But not so in business. The uniqueness of each person is seldom acknowledged, though meaningless clichés, such as 'people are important in our business', abound. Anita Roddick of Body Shop talks disparagingly of company chairmen who talk of 'the people in our company are our greatest asset'. As she says, 'People aren't an asset – people *are* the company'. Seeing them as assets is like seeing customers as consumers. It dehumanizes them.

Performers work in an environment where individual differences are not seen as an annoyance or an obstacle to planning. Audiences clamour to see the individual contribution a particular actor, opera singer, concert pianist, or dancer can bring to a role or a piece of music.

> **" The hardest battle is to be nobody but yourself in a world, which is doing its best, night and day to make you everybody else. "**
>
> *e. e. cummings*

Using each person's unique talent is a way of life in the performing arts. We shall be exploring how business can build this approach into its own teams.

Developing trust

In the theatre, developing trust is a starting point for all successful team efforts. Many business teams discover the need to build trust far too late, for example when the team is under-performing or in crisis.

Confronted with a need to build trust, how does business respond? One way has been to send people climbing mountains or down potholes together. If you have been dangling at the end of a rope held by a colleague, surely you automatically develop trust. Sadly, though, on return to the work place this type of trust frequently vanishes. It's hard to translate the outdoor experience into the ordinary work place. By contrast, the development of trust within a performing arts team is part of the normal, collective team experience.

Because the performing arts so regularly need a trusting environment, they have developed many interesting and useful ways of achieving it. We shall be exploring later some of these. It is merely important to note here the ease with which the performing arts develop an environment in which people feel safe to express themselves, to challenge the status quo and to make a creative contribution. Such experience is a valuable resource on which open-minded business people can readily draw in order to achieve more powerful teams.

Unlocking personal energy

The amount of sheer energy available within a successful team from the performing arts is astonishing. Long hours, intensive work, few breaks and often physically gruelling activity are common. Everyone understands the price of success requires enormous energy.

Where does this apparently boundless energy come from? Are people in the performing arts physically fitter or more active than the rest of us? There is no real evidence to support that idea.

What makes a successful performing arts team such an energetic place to work in, is its ability to unlock each person's own store of personal energy. That only happens when people feel it will be used properly and fully valued. It is also encouraged when team leaders understand the processes for releasing this invaluable resource.

Within business teams, personal energy is usually taken for granted. There is seldom much effort, for example, to raise energy levels consciously, and there is often a poor awareness of when individual and team energy levels are low, and little idea what to do about it. Since the performing arts have developed useful ways to liberate personal energy, for the benefit of both the team and the individual, they are a resource for business to draw upon.

Learning from the performing arts

We have briefly looked at some key factors that the performing arts do well: *building commitment, generating excitement, being creative, using each person's unique talent, developing trust, unlocking personal energy.* Since these are all required in business too, especially in a recessionary climate, it is time to wake up to what the performing arts have to offer. All it takes is a willingness to do things differently. As the head of IBM, BP, General Motors or whoever once said: 'Go on doing what you've always done and you wind up with the same as you've always had'.

Translating the special assets of the creative and performing arts into workable tools for practising managers has been under way for some years. These assets have, for instance, been playing an increasingly important role in the field of business training. Videos, distance learning, role plays and computer-based training have all borrowed heavily from the performing arts.

Drama and the performing arts have an important place in our society. We might reasonably expect therefore that they would have an important role within all our major institutions, including businesses. Not so. Generally our cultural heritage is consigned to theatres, studios and museums. We are poorer as a result.

Within business the shift in recent years away from excessive rationalism has not simply been a rejection of a sterile hunt for certainties. It has also reflected a hunger for a richer diet, a recognition that our great corporations and human enterprises cannot survive and flourish solely on numbers and computer printouts.

For business organizations to mature and prosper into and beyond the year 2000, our cultural traditions must be more fully incorporated into how we run these enterprises. They are the heart and soul of successful companies. Many people, for example, have noted the similarities between retail shops and theatre, management and performance, boardroom life and drama.

This does not mean that all managers must take up amateur dramatics, though many of them already do that, or that every work place must be filled with paintings and sculptures, though that too is happening in some places. We even heard of one manager in a major communications company who keeps a piano in his office!

The challenge that we see is how the average business person or busy manager can learn to incorporate our cultural tradition of the performing arts into the ordinary working environment. Rejecting the arts as irrelevant to running a business is to cut ourselves off from a vital part of our heritage and the source of exceptional results.

Unused potential

Our basic assumptions behind ACE teams are simple:

- Most people at work have much unused potential.
- People are willing to devote effort, and to risk and explore what it will take to use their full potential.
- The ordinary manager or business leader can tap into people's potential and, by releasing it, produce exceptional results.

Some outstanding managers or successful entrepreneurs already realize how to do this. Yet we reject the idea that only the charismatic leaders, the high profile personalities like John Harvey Jones, Lee Iaccocca or Graham Day can inspire their followers. If that were the case then most organizations could never hope to have exceptional teams.

" Powerlessness corrupts. And absolute powerlessness corrupts absolutely. "

Rosabeth Moss Kanter

The potential for exceptional teams exists in most enterprises. Research we conducted among a number of representative companies revealed many employees felt their potential was significantly under used. Thus an important question which many business leaders need to ask is:

- 'What will it take to unlock that potential?'

As you might expect, the answer is not to merely continue doing what has always been done before.

The creative and performing arts are demanding to be heard. Not because they are paragons of organizational efficiency – there are some appalling examples of bad business practices and poor people management! We are not suggesting the performing arts have *all* the answers. They don't. Instead we have selected carefully – looking at the best that goes on in the arts. Adapting them to business use is what the rest of this book is all about.

" Working with the Animals rock group was like a stage coach with horses at the four corners. "

Alan Price

Where do you start building a team? Team-building experts suggest groups usually pass through a process of birth, adolescence, middle age, senility and death. Another way of viewing this is a process of FORMING, STORMING, NORMING, PERFORMING AND MOURNING. However, these merely describe what may occur, they hardly show how to make the various stages happen or to speed them up. As our managing director in the opening dialogue asks, faced with the task of creating a star performing team, what do you do? Or if you have an established team and have to raise it to the next level of performance, where do you start?

Throughout ACE teams there are ideas transferrable to the realities of the business environment. We offer numerous suggestions for actions you can actually *do* to make a difference. How many you try depends on how much of a difference you want to make. To create star performance, you will probably need a complete shift in approach. It could be an exciting adventure.

Ace teams

The famous research by Meredith Belbin (*Management Teams*, Butterworth-Heinemann) on why management teams succeed and fail suggested there were certain key roles winning teams possessed. So, for example, a successful management team would have eight roles, such as a company worker, a chairman, a shaper and so on.

We do not quarrel with such findings, only argue that in the winning teams we have encountered such roles are never rigid. Everyone has the potential to play each one as the occasion requires. In fact the moment a team really sparks and functions at a highly productive level, the conventional roles often break down. At these moments something else is happening. Something very special is going on – and conventional research doesn't begin to explain it.

So many problems in companies stem from poor teamwork that we no longer take it at face value when people say 'We work really well together'. On delving into such situations we have been impressed by how often people later reveal that they feel their individual and group potential is under-used.

So what is a truly exceptional team? Is it one that produces the bottom line results of exceptional profits? Or in the public sector one that offers outstanding service? Certainly these are some of the signs. Yet often a team needs to be exceptional long before the results appear as end of term marks, like profits or service, or a project finished on time.

Truly exceptional teams – star performers – are:

ALIGNED, CREATIVE and EXPLORING

We have adapted these principles from the performing arts where teams regularly achieving outstanding results in weeks or months, rather than years. Let us see how business can also start creating ACE teams.

FOR LATECOMERS

The curtain rose on the two pressing issues of how to produce exceptional teams quickly and what lessons the peforming arts can offer in this area.

Diversity and the changing nature of teams were spotlighted, with the increasing requirement for teams to be star performers.

Exceptional teams were shown to need an effort to build commitment, generate excitement, be creative, use each person's unique talent, develop trust and unlock personal energy.

The three assumptions behind ACE teams were explained and the need for a new approach to building teams was presented.

An exceptional team was defined as one that is a star performer, and is Aligned, Creative and Exploring.

These principles were adapted from the performing arts and provide the basis for the rest of the show.

Act One:
ALIGNED

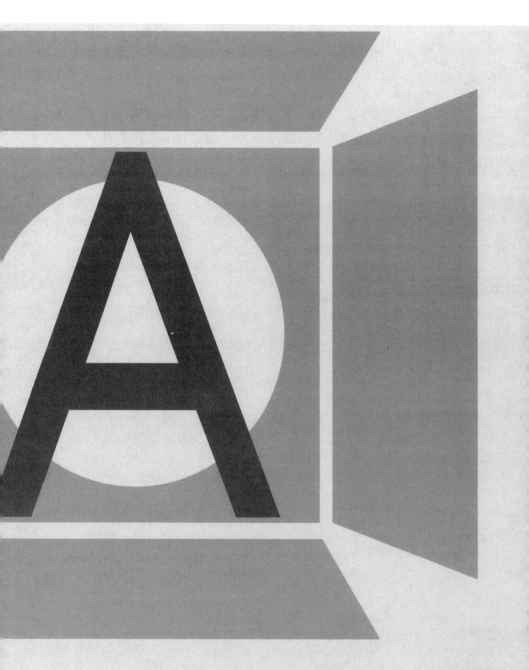

Act One: **ALIGNED**

PROLOGUE

PROLOGUE

" The power of a waterfall is nothing but a lot of drips working together. "

Aligned: falling into line; allied; alliance

At Stonehenge, Avebury or Carnac you will see the alignments of standing stones. They are clear and powerful symbols of agreed objectives. We may not fully grasp the nature of those objectives, yet the sense of agreed purpose and alignment shines through.

An ACE team too is strongly aligned. It knows where it's going; even when unclear about precisely how to get there. Question the team members or talk to those who have regular dealings with them and you quickly detect a sense of joint purpose.

The foundation stone of an exceptional team is always alignment, and the best in the performing arts always invest time and emotional energy to achieve it. They realize that from this agreed sense of purpose springs creative energy and confidence to extend the team's own boundaries. Alignment does not require everyone to like each other however, nor does it necessarily prevent strong disagreements. Many successful teams are aligned almost despite themselves.

One of the great creative partnerships in British musical tradition, Gilbert and Sullivan, could hardly be called cosy. They were often rude to each other and frequently refused even to meet. Their exceptional results arose from being strongly aligned as a team for concentrated periods. We can only speculate what they might have achieved with even more prolonged alignment.

Most business teams take alignment for granted. 'We're a great team' is a commonly heard claim. When it is true, you find the team has consciously invested as much energy as any performing arts team achieving alignment.

Frequently, though, it's a mistake to take alignment for granted. We recently worked with the board of a company that seemed well aligned. Each director was asked privately to list the three current major objectives facing the company – a sort of secret ballot. The results were a shock to them all. The so-called team differed widely on what they thought most needed doing; alignment had yet to be achieved, partly explaining why progress was slow.

Are we aligned?

How would you recognize an aligned team? You could look at its results, but then this is often too late. Or you could attempt to assess whether the members are using their full potential as human beings. However, we need other indicators to assess the team's health, and identify whether or how to improve alignment.

Aligned teams work at certain important tasks that make their members into a focused force for change:

- Leadership.
- Organization.
- Relationships.
- Personal investment.

These are risky areas, since they concern behaviour with and towards other people, and important choices and commitments. These areas are 'messy', hard to measure and depend on interpersonal skills; no wonder so many managers see them as a headache and prefer to avoid them.

Yet business teams need to work on them to reach alignment. With limited experience of such risk-taking, some companies have struggled to find ways to explore it. We've already mentioned the lengths to which managers and employees will go to generate such team spirit. They abseil down cliffs, hike over mountains, canoe through rapids, plunge down potholes, or shoot one another with paint pellets. While these do sometimes produce alignment, they may also create interesting side-effects.

People often return from the experience more in tune with nature and the excitement of the outdoors than with the team. Others decide that their existing job, employer or the team is the wrong one for them; or back at work they find difficulty in relating the learning to the real work.

Performing arts teams though have found ways to create risky experiences that enable them to explore alignment in a safe and challenging way, yet one that is totally work-related.

Act One therefore explores the four challenges facing a team seeking alignment:

SCENE 1   'ONCE MORE UNTO THE BREACH' – Aligned leadership
SCENE 2   'WHOSE LINE IS IT ANYWAY?' – Incisive organization
SCENE 3   'WHO CARES WINS!' – Supportive relationships
SCENE 4   'THE ANGEL FACTOR' – Personal investment

"Leadership is like beauty, it's hard to define, but you know it when you see it."

Warren Bennis

Scene 1 - **'ONCE MORE UNTO THE BREACH'**

Aligned Leadership

Aligned Leadership

The conversation continues, as our two protagonists struggle with the issues of team-building:

MANAGING DIRECTOR:	*I can see we have a lot in common. I thought we'd be miles apart, but we are, to use your word, quite aligned. Mind you, we are both directors, after all.*
THEATRE DIRECTOR:	*Yes, we're both supposed to provide a sense of direction – but your title has always rather bothered me.*
MANAGING DIRECTOR:	*What d'you mean?*
THEATRE DIRECTOR:	*I've always thought that managing was a bit of a misnomer, when what's really needed is leadership.*
MANAGING DIRECTOR:	*Interesting you should say that. Just the other day my colleagues were discussing the difference between managers and leaders.*
THEATRE DIRECTOR:	*Yes. Managing has always implied to me a sense of 'just about coping'. You know, somebody asks how you're doing and you say 'I'm managing'. Not exactly inspiring, is it?*
MANAGING DIRECTOR:	*Well, what about your world?*
THEATRE DIRECTOR:	*No one really talks about leaders or managers. Look at orchestras, for example. Even though the first violinist is called the leader, it's the conductor, out front, who really provides the direction. Dance companies have choreographers, in my own field it's artistic directors, and in TV and radio it's directors and producers. And on a film set the director is called any number of things including boss, guv'nor, chief and a lot more less polite!*
MANAGING DIRECTOR:	*Sounds familiar.*
THEATRE DIRECTOR:	*I'm sure. However, the managing is done by administrators. Vital though they are, we wouldn't look to them for inspirational leadership.*
MANAGING DIRECTOR:	*So what's in a name? It's not the title that matters, it's what they do that's important. I mean, I agree*

	with the need for leadership but it's what the leaders do that's important, surely, not what they're called.
THEATRE DIRECTOR:	*Couldn't agree more. So what exactly do we do, d'you reckon?*
MANAGING DIRECTOR:	*With or without teams, I think our job is to start things – you know, initiate them. And to transform things – loss into profit, machinery into productivity, ideas into fruition, people into a team. You know what I mean?*
THEATRE DIRECTOR:	*Absolutely. That's what we do all the time. It's perfectly normal. Plays, scripts, sketches, musical manuscripts are forever being converted into hopefully brilliant human performances. For that to happen, teams need to have a common sense of purpose, a vision, shared values and clarity of leadership.*
MANAGING DIRECTOR:	*In other words – alignment.*
THEATRE DIRECTOR:	*Exactly.*
MANAGING DIRECTOR:	*But that takes time. In my experience to get a team to that level can take months.*
THEATRE DIRECTOR:	*Yes . . . and no. It normally takes me about 20 minutes on the first day of rehearsal to get the team aligned about our shared vision.*
MANAGING DIRECTOR:	*20 minutes? Lead on, I want to hear more!*

Leadership

> " **Leadership is like beauty, it's hard to define, but you know it when you see it.** "
>
> *Warren Bennis*

Team leadership matters far more in our Western society these days, because people no longer give blind obedience. 'You're lucky to work here, do as you're told' is a thing of the past. Try behaving at work like the dictatorial Frederick the Great, or even that once archetypal manager Alfred Sloane of General Motors, and today's most talented subordinates would leave. Even in the 1960–80s managers had greater power over their subordinates than today. They were under less pressure to find ways of drawing the best from each individual for the benefit of the entire team.

Now a growing number of employees expect a climate in which freedom and self-expression flourish. For instance, a 1990 MORI poll found that over 70 per cent of those at work sought 'greater involvement with their organizations'.

Take one of London's leading hotels, for example, where we ran a workshop for the thirty-five top managers. This five-star watering hole, with one of the grandest London views, was once among the most fashionable spots to stay while in the capital. Now it had faded, and was surviving in increasingly shark-infested waters. Five other comparable hotels now plied for trade nearby, while yet another was being lovingly crafted, with money no object, in a converted listed building.

Many of the hotel's top managers were still mentally living in an earlier, cosier era, expecting their staff to blindly follow instructions. To regain its reputation, the hotel needed a new climate, in which everyone, including the cleaners, chambermaids and doormen, would contribute more openly, creatively, and with new self-expression.

Fortunately they appointed a new general manager, who leapt at the chance of aligning the team. He asked us to work with each department, so that their managers saw their interdependence. No longer would they be separate little empires, doing their own thing, but, instead, a team of department heads all working for the same end and going in the same direction.

An example of the kind of leadership we mean occurs in a successful dance group or a leading repertory company. All members are expected to be true to their own creative integrity, able to express themselves, while still feeling part of a tightly knit group with a common aim. Leadership in these circumstances is so difficult that those doing it well have developed experience that is transferable to all organizations.

Michael Diacono, Managing Director of United Magazine Distribution, was marvelling at how conductors or theatre directors lead:

I am amazed at what they do. I believe *I* manage my team pretty well, but let's face it, they're a disciplined bunch, ready and willing to follow my lead. But when you think of actors and musicians ... their whole philosophy is about individuality and freedom. They're trying to break the rules all the time and come up with something new. To harness that sort of chaotic energy must take incredible powers of leadership. And what's more, they do it so quickly. They have to weld all those disparate creative elements into a team in a matter of hours, not weeks and months as in business.

Trying to improve leadership is now on the agenda of most forward-thinking companies. Many have tried training courses. These mainly teach management. Leaders invent themselves and are not made in a weekend seminar. You have to learn leadership through practice, rather than be taught it. Becoming a leader is really the same as becoming yourself. What this means is that real leaders worry less about proving themselves than how they can express themselves.

When we ask business teams 'What is the leader's role?', a common answer is 'to motivate people'. It's something you do to other people. We see it differently. The crucial issue is *inspiration*.

You can tell inspiration is an unfamiliar idea to business people when so many look uncomfortable on hearing it. Our suggestion to managers that 'your job is to inspire people' is commonly greeted with silence or some extremely worried expressions. Yet it's the clearest dividing line between a manager and a leader.

INSPIRATION

" He inspired in us the belief that we were working in a
medium that was powerful enough to influence the
whole world. "

Lillian Gish, on D. W. Griffiths

To inspire others start with
yourself.

Begin by listing some items or things
that make you feel happy or uplifted in
some way: poems, pictures, films,
objects, novels, encounters, events,
people.

Share these with the team and ask
them to do the same.

Have inspirational items around the
work place – in the office, at reception,
even in the toilets! Change them
regularly, so they remain fresh and
always generate conversation.

People become so much more
inspiring when they get in touch with
what makes them personally feel that
way.

Inspiring leaders can make practically
anything happen. The challenge for
business leaders is learning how to do
it. It happens regularly in the best stage
companies, dance groups, film
companies because:

- The leader has a vision.
- The leader talks about the vision -
  constantly.

Vision

It's almost impossible for a theatre or opera
director to start work without first having a
vision for the finished production. They
will describe this imaginative scheme and
then collaborate with the cast to achieve it.
Sometimes it's a fully fledged vision,

complete to the last detail. Usually it's only partial, difficult to grasp and needing more clarity. That's when teamwork really counts.

" The thing has already taken form in my mind before I start it. "

Vincent Van Gogh

A team can help articulate the vision, and in doing so begins to be inspired. It happened in the 1960s, for example, when Peter Brook produced a revolutionary version of Shakespeare's *A Midsummer Night's Dream*. He kept telling the cast they were releasing something in the play never seen before. He made huge demands, asking them to do exercises they had never attempted, like learning circus skills such as trapeze work and juggling. Their questioning, challenging and personal development during the whole exhausting process pushed Brook further on too. Together they fumbled towards a breakthrough.

What kept them going was Brook's visionary insistence they could reveal a new dimension of the play. His commitment inspired and galvanized. You may think it bizarre having trapezes and juggling in a hallowed Shakespeare play. While you can quarrel with the interpretation, Brook certainly found a different perspective, and people loved the results.

> Everyone can have a vision. Who cares if at the beginning it's woolly and ill formed?
>
> Start with even the vaguest dream and invite others to help firm it up and suggest ways of making it a reality. They'll have fun and may soon be hooked.

The arts are by no means alone in the exploitation of vision. Most organizations these days talk about it, along with mission statements. The difference is that in the arts it has always been higher on the agenda. Performers know it is virtually impossible to move forward without the whole team focusing on and aligning behind a vision.

Many commercial companies, realizing the need for a clear vision, also now experience the exhaustive process of creating one. The senior management team of the Sun Life Assurance Company, for instance, spent many intense meetings trying to arrive at a vision that expressed where they were going. It started as a series of disconnected ideas, before being honed down into a coherent imaginative statement.

" The seeds of our success grow through our customer commitment, cultivating our staff and weeding out the companion. "

Mission Statement of Badshot Lea Garden Centre

Our Vision

Sun*Life*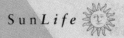

Sun Life aims to be the leading life assurance, pensions and investment company in all our chosen market sectors. We will meet our customers' needs for protection, security and investment growth and will seek to achieve total customer satisfaction through continuous improvement of our products, performance and service.

Sun*Service*

We will be **distinctive** by understanding and meeting our customers' needs in three areas:

Superior **Solutions**
* Using technical and financial expertise to create outstanding products and services.

Superior **Service**
* Delivering a fast, friendly and fault-free service, second to none in the industry.

Superior **Satisfaction**
* Delivering consistently superior investment performance and providing efficient administration at below industry average cost.

Sun*Spirit*

We will each deliver this **commitment to industry excellence** by:-

* Putting the customer first at all times.
* Taking individual responsibility to satisfy customer needs.
* Maximising opportunities for self-development.
* Creating an environment of professionalism, integrity and fun.
* Valuing teamwork as the means to attain our objectives.
* Seeking continuous improvement in all our operations.
* Taking pride in Sun Life.

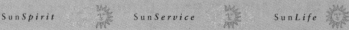

Sun*Spirit*   Sun*Service*   Sun*Life*

We worked with the members of the executive in communicating this vision to the rest of the company. They were speaking at conferences up and down the country. We were constantly reminding them of that initial creative process where they had become excited at the prospect of the future success of the company. If they could communicate *that* to the workforce, then they really would be on the way to realizing their vision.

The power of vision to sustain and direct a team onwards and upwards cannot be entirely explained. However, it undoubtedly works. Most successful business have begun with a powerful vision, and most fail when the vision fades.

The creation of the outstanding distribution company Federal Express happened, for instance, because of founder Fred Smith's vision of distribution as a central point with a hub and the lines of distribution as spokes radiating from the centre. The wheel image was not itself revolutionary, for at least three freight services had tried it as early as the 1930s. Smith's vision was to do it on a huge scale, and while his competitors too had access to the same vision, somehow they never saw it.

In 1980 another wild man, Ted Turner, was even more outrageous, following his loony vision of what critics labelled the Chicken Noodle Network – for CNN, or Cable News Network. It was the laughing stock of every media commentator. They predicted his rapid downfall but, instead, his 24-hour news network became the most influential broadcast news source in the United States. The White House, the Pentagon and foreign embassies, let alone millions of homes in America, were soon constantly tuned to CNN. Today CNN is beamed to countless countries and homes. This was literally vision in action.

> Recall your personal experience of visions that have been realized – past successes and triumphs when imagined ideas have been achieved. No matter if these seem trivial compared to the great works of others. Just choose those times when your vision came true.
>
> With those in mind, go and look for what isn't there, what isn't happening, what might be. You are looking for things that might be better or different.
>
> Start conversations with colleagues to practise articulating your vision – however vague. It will help the team to refine the vision.

Having a vision is not enough to lead a team well. Creating visions is relatively easy, even ones that excite other people. Look at any book on generating creative ideas and in a few hours or even minutes you will probably arrive at some unusual and often important new possibilities. The real skill, though, is in turning them into a reality.

> The famous art director John Box came out of retirement to work on a film. He explained his decision in this way: 'I spent half an hour talking to the director, and I wanted to be part of his vision'.

Enrolment is the essential process for moving from vision to a programme of action. You can have visions till the cows come home; it is not enough. People have to say 'Yes, I want to be part of making that happen too'.

So how are people enrolled? It doesn't have to take months, it can be done in a few dynamic minutes – just watch theatre people at it! Top directors talk to set and costume designers, sound and lighting people, the stage assistants and the actors. They go on talking, listening, sharing, until everyone concerned with the production has a sense of their vision. On the first day of rehearsal models of the set design and drawings of costumes are shown and discussed – anything that will help everyone to imagine the vision as a reality. They are often greeted with 'Ooohs' and 'Aaahs', always with great interest. It's the start of turning the ideas into action.

DISSENTING VOICE

" **My professor told me when I started in the 40's that a director should listen and keep his mouth shut. Took me a long time to understand I talked too much. Now I know you should listen with your ears – and your heart.** "

Ingmar Bergman

Before sending his team off to work on a film Walt Disney would stand and tell the entire story to them. He held them spellbound for hours, doing the funny voices and acting all the parts. He made his vision so alive that even his sometimes sceptical colleagues concluded 'I want to be part of making this happen'.

After expressing an interest in Richard Attenborough's dream of making the film *Gandhi*, Jake Eberts of Goldcrest Films found 'within minutes Dickie was in my office, giving me what was to be the first of many brilliant and emotional performances, acting out every role and dancing around on his surprisingly nimble feet, re-creating scenes and events in the script – all with such enthusiasm and energy that, even if I had any doubts, I would have been won over'.

Other directors do it differently. Regardless of how it's done, performance teams live through their shared vision. It inspires them to aim for the best. With a strong vision, people just get on with it. It is no wonder employees in so many places feel lost or disillusioned. Who tells them the story, gets them excited, inspires them about the

Have you a vision for your team?
Instead of trying to describe it, draw it!
In the space opposite scribble, sketch or craft a cartoon, an icon, a symbol, a drawing of any kind, that somehow conveys or symbolizes your vision. No one need see it at this stage; just don't use any words.
  Pictures often tell us more than we realize about what we are thinking.

future? When somebody does, the effect is electric – people do tasks without being directed; they take responsibility for helping to make it happen.

Find creative ways of communicating your vision. Talk enthusiastically about it within your team and beyond it.

Have vision statements displayed on desks, walls and in literature. Find a visual way of representing the vision – a symbol, logo or object - and use the image on notepaper and memo pads, etc.

Try using metaphors to express what you are talking about. Darwin used the branches of a tree to explain his vision of evolution, William James described the mental process as a stream or river, and John Locke adopted the falconer whose release of a bird symbolized the quest for human knowledge. In one company we worked with they adopted a spoon as their new metaphor to symbolize the fact that from now on things were really going to be stirred up!

To enrol people in the vision, help them turn it into theirs.

British-owned Hilton International (part of Ladbroke Group PLC) runs a training programme called 'The Hilton Promise', where staff at all levels set measurable standards of performance that they personally intend to achieve.

Compare this to the many companies in which the standards are imposed as directives from above.

The London Bubble Theatre Company has a vision of giving exciting, accessible shows to people who normally never visit the theatre. Every member of that company, from the person running the box office to the community liaison officer, from a performer to the administrator, knows what they do actively contributes to the vision of that organization. No wonder they are inspired! One of the company's products, a musical called *Return to the Forbidden Planet*, transferred to the West End, Broadway and Australia. A vision can be highly profitable if converted into action through successful enrolment.

Teams often start with a clear sense of vision and yet sometimes lose momentum. A vision is by definition **what is not there now**. One is struggling to reach for what is missing, to bring it into existence. Thus the need to keep talking about it, to share it and to keep reinforcing it. One of the most powerful ways of reinforcing a vision that has been used by both individuals and teams is what we call the film show.

For a decade Richard Attenborough dreamed and schemed about making a blockbuster film about Gandhi. During all that time he kept trying to enrol people in his vision – always talking about it. What sustained him? Over the years he kept running the film through his head, seeing it until for him it was so real that he could convince others it was a reality too.

In the film show one keeps running the vision through one's head just like Richard Attenborough and his Gandhi project. You keep playing a mental picture of how the vision would look if it came into existence. In a company you might imagine what true excellence would look like and 'watch' a scene in which it manifested itself.

Effective leaders are running the film show in their heads all the time, though they may not always know they're doing it. But what about a team? How does it watch the film show? A good way is to tell stories about what the vision would look and feel like if it became real. Another way is to write scenarios and act them out. Along these lines we developed an innovative workshop called 'The Producers', in which the team creates a series of videos about its vision and uses them to identify practical action for making it happen.

The essential point is the continuous need to work at expressing and firming up the vision. The process helps achieve team alignment. As the Hollywood producer and acting teacher Dan Fauci says, 'If you haven't got a vision, get one. If it's unclear, get clear. If you've got one, expand it!'

Values

"If you want to add value to your business, you've got to add values."

HRH the Prince of Wales, addressing members of Business in the Community

What enrols people in the vision is not just the excitement, it is the values that lie behind it. People who share values are aligned as a team. That happened in a well-respected theatre company called Shared Experience. As the name implies, the members formed the company because they wanted an evening in the theatre to be just that – a shared experience between performers and audience. What they most valued about their vision was **the spontaneous relationship between actor and audience**.

Everyone employed by the company fully understood the implications – no reliance on theatrical artifice, nothing that could get in the way of pursuing their core value. Company members always invited the audience to join them to create the evening's entertainment. Every team member wanted to make this happen.

Their name clarified and communicated their values, as did their brochures, programmes and promotional literature. The single message was clear. No pomp and ceremony, no grandeur, just an honest sharing of creative powers. The actors welcomed the audience into the auditorium and showed them to their seats. The whole cast were on stage all the time and everything that happened did so in full view. The company thrived because each member of the team was totally committed to a shared set of clearly identified values, which they communicated both internally and externally.

When a team is successfully turning its vision into action, you will see how **values align the team behind its vision**. Interestingly, business is finally arriving at exactly this view. In the early 1990s the Harvard Business School conducted a huge survey of 12,000 managers in twenty-five countries, asking them what were the new management realities and how they were facing up to them. The core issue to emerge was the importance and central role of values, or, as Professor Moss Kanter put it, 'In a world of growing de-centralisation, values are important as corporate glue. They give coherence, and compatible decisions are made'.

Although some people wake in the morning with a clear vision in their mind's eye of what could be, it is more usually expressed as **a deeply held set of values**. That is why teams need to test what their values are, for they are the stepping stones to a realized vision.

ACE teams that produce star performances therefore:

- Clarify values.
- Commit to values.
- Communicate values.
- Convert values to action.

In setting up our own company we spent a considerable time attempting to clarify corporate values. Producing a corporate brochure turned out to be less important for what it said than the experience of nailing down what we were really about and how to encapsulate it.

Among the values we initially listed were waking people up, helping people have fun and grow, enhancing creativity, helping people become inspired. After vigorous debates we became clearer that our core value was **unlocking people's potential**. That's what we cared about most, and it would sustain and nurture us through the commercial minefield of starting a company in the middle of a recession.

It was not totally original and some might say too slick, yet it summed up what mattered most to us. Recently when someone was mildly critical of it as 'old hat', we agreed, yet the striving we had experienced ensured its resilience in the face of critical comment. It remains our core value.

Clarifying core values is a journey of discovery. Theatre companies do it all the time. When they start to rehearse, they do not aim for a pedestrian production. They strive for outstanding performance yet may have only a vague notion of how this value can be realized.

Sadly, lack of clarity about values means that what a team cares about may stay hidden and prove destructive. For example, we see teams that declare they value excellence yet treat one another in shoddy ways. Others say they value innovation yet greet new ideas with 'Yes, but . . .' and a barrage of excuses.

When values have been clarified they invariably turn out to be people-centred, expressed and communicated through people's behaviour. People do not just talk about values, they act them out. You can see values in action. They are qualitative rather than quantifiable: you do not run a measure over a value and read off the results on a scale. Yet they are clearly present.

" Working in a Body Shop is a bit like being in a show – it's a performance, and so we want people who are actors and actresses and like to perform. These are the values I admire. "

Anita Roddick

However, before devising a whole new set of values that the team want to work with, have a look at what already exists. You will see that the values will be there. Whether the team has consciously chosen them or not, they will be hidden away in the culture, the relationships and the everyday actions of the group.

Drawing out the team's true values is hard, straight questioning may not work. An alternative route is to review . . .

'What really seems to matter to us in this team?'

Values are usually deeply rooted, and while writing them down is useful, it may not make much real impact. It is only too easy to come up with a list of values as if that will automatically achieve results. National Power, for example, did an excellent job in listing important company values as follows:

- We will value our customers.
  We are determined to provide an excellent and responsive service that makes us the preferred supplier.
- We will value our shareholders.
  We are determined to produce a performance that sustains their confidence in the company.
- We will value our staff,
  promoting initiative and rewarding achievement.
- We will care for the environment.
  We have pledged to safeguard it.

Many people, watching rising prices, the escalating salaries of National Power's managers, the growing criticisms of environmental and monopoly abuse, would want to question the company's real commitment to its stated values.

Try asking your team 'What do you think are our hidden values - or what seems to really matter to us?'
If the answer is something like . . .

> Honesty
> Hard work
> Respect for talent
> Company morale
> Staff retention
> Customer service
> Accuracy of work
> Optimum pay

. . . it might be worth making these explicit and acknowledging them as shared values.
  However, you should start to worry if you arrive at a list such as . . .

> Minimizing pay
> Autocratic leadership
> Keeping to the rules
> Covering your back
> Avoiding mistakes
> Eliminating risks
> Staying out of trouble
> Not losing face

Commitment to values

Many companies talk of being 'market-, sales- or profit driven'. How about one that is 'values-driven'? The idea works for many charitable organizations, where there is seldom a problem preserving staff enthusiasm. The same goes for the performing arts, where, despite all the pressure and lack of financial rewards, people commit themselves wholeheartedly to the chosen values.

So, what is commitment? Paradoxically it's often used as a common excuse for being unable to take action. 'No, sorry, I can't do that, I have other commitments.' So instead of being an asset, commitment becomes a millstone.

True commitment is the opposite of a millstone. It stems from having and making a choice about a task. You give your word to be committed and work for it. Not forever – nothing is written in blood – but just as long as the task remains unfinished. If you change your mind and choose something else, people need to be told about your change in commitment.

Partial commitment is more difficult to handle than no commitment at all. If you are fully committed to a ski-jump, losing weight, giving a presentation, completing a project, introducing a change, your whole energy is behind it. Nothing holds you back. When you are only 60 per cent committed, it becomes hard work, since 40 per cent of your energy is pulling in the opposite direction.

People's level of commitment is soon obvious when team values are clear. Clarity also helps pinpoint where blockages to commitment exist and what might be done about them.

In a major security company we worked with, for example, the information technology department wanted improvement in the team's performance. After exploring core values, the IT group identified a need for the rest of the department's several hundred staff to help in raising the quality of service. But one member of the team, who headed the important computer operations room, explained how difficult it would be, how work pressures would prevent him making progress, how his computer operators were too busy running the machines and so on. For him the change proposed would indeed be a struggle. There was little chance of creating an aligned, ACE team with such half-hearted commitment.

Since they had spent nearly a day identifying quality of service as a value they most wanted to pursue more vigorously, nearly everyone was keen to define an action plan. But the operations manager expressed yet more doubts and could not offer a full commitment. The team soon realized it would be tough to achieve their aim when an important contributor would be continually using his energy in a negative way. After further efforts to gain his commitment without success, he and the team parted company.

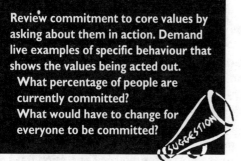

Review commitment to core values by asking about them in action. Demand live examples of specific behaviour that shows the values being acted out.
What percentage of people are currently committed?
What would have to change for everyone to be committed?

Communicating the values

People often feel reluctant to spend time talking about values because they seem vague or metaphysical. Yet talking about them is essential and makes it easier for people to identify with them.

Those who do office jobs for a ballet or opera company or are cleaners for an orchestra or secretaries in a theatre group normally watch the company performances. They can see what they contribute to the values of the organization.

If you work in manufacturing, you may never see the finished product. People spent years making Rolls-Royces, for example, supposedly one of the best cars in the world, yet many of them had never even driven in one. When you work in IT, research, administration, technical support, or accounts, you may never really see the results of your labour and have no easy starting point for talking about values. It is a creative challenge for team leaders to find ways for people to identify with the values that underpin the vision.

Within Body Shop there are non-stop communications producing internal videos and newsletters. The company also uses the products to advertise values, puts posters in the shops and plasters its lorries with slogans. From the receptionist to the seasoned PR professional, from the person on the production line to the training specialist, everyone is bursting to talk to you. They all want to convey the Body Shop message, to sell the values to you, explain what they are doing and show you how it all works.

At Apple computers, every 'mouse' pad has the company's values on it.

Converting values into performance

" After all is said and done – more is said than done. "

We convert values into action by living them out. Some of the disasters associated with Total Quality Management (TQM), for example, have occurred through launching schemes on a barrage of rhetoric, backed up with inadequate action. The most obvious instance we have seen is where a management adopted total quality as a value it wanted to promote and introduced it to staff in crowded, smoke-filled, uncomfortable rooms. No wonder people left feeling cynical about quality.

Business has something to learn from the theatre in this area. We mentioned earlier the London Bubble Theatre, which seeks to create productions and workshops that are accessible and entertaining, and that attract new audiences to the theatre. Underpinning this goal is a set of values that shows up in the actions of all the team. Seat prices are low and even the auditorium expresses the values. It's a tent.

> **Explore how 'values-driven' you are.**
> Be willing to discuss values regularly, not just at a once a year jamboree.
> Check for signs of values being practised - in the working environment, relationships, product and organization.
>
> (SUGGESTION)

How does a tent express a theatre's values? In the early 1970s, when the company began, its members were aware that non-theatregoers found West End Theatres inhibiting and stuffy. So the London Bubble tours in a tent, erecting it in local parks – more like a circus, yet reflecting the company's stated value of 'reflecting the needs of the community'.

A good example of a business that really has turned its values into action is the National Freight Corporation. In 1979 the ailing NFC was the first state-owned operation on the government's hit list for privatization. Sir Peter Thompson and his team came up with a revolutionary idea: the management and employees between them should buy the company. Eight years later, when they floated the company on the Stock Market, a lorry driver who had originally invested £500 then owned shares worth £50,000.

The company continues its commitment to employee ownership as its Shareholders Annual Report shows. Its core values are shown on the next page.

It was an arduous journey to achieve NFC's success, but it did it. It made Sir Peter Thompson's idea happen to the benefit of all the teams in the organization.

Converting values into performance requires tangible steps, not vague generalizations. And that demands clear leadership.

It's always worth asking a team about a task:

• Who is going to make sure it happens?

Whether there are different people for different projects or the same person supervising the whole task, a clear leader is essential. They could be called project manager, product champion, co-ordinator, facilitator, manager, director or boss – who cares, just *as long as somebody owns it!*
  Secondly:

• Can the task be summed up in one sentence?

We recently came across a set of objectives given to a computer project team of a large financial services company. The only person who understood it was their leader. His team of experts had to read the document five or six times to see what he was getting at.

Clarity of leadership

The famous remark 'I must follow them; I am their leader', attributed to various great leaders, reflects the often paradoxical nature of leadership. Are you supposed to show the way and take a team with you? Or get the team to clarify and own its vision and go with it?

The truth is there is no simple answer. Everyone leads in different ways. The single most important factor, though, is being clear about what is going on. Who is leading at any one time, and how? Who takes responsibility for seeing the team convert its values into action? Let's look at an orchestra.

When a conductor stands on the podium, there is total clarity about who will guide the creative event about to happen. Although there is also the 'leader' of the orchestra – the first violinist – the chain of command is clear and the shared responsibilities obvious to all. The clarity is similar to that which should exist in business, say, between chairman and managing director, or departmental head and line manager.

Problems arise when people are unsure who is guiding the creative event. One of the major reasons for the financial difficulties that afflicted the Dutch multinational Philips company in recent years was said to be a plethora of subsidiary companies. The heads of the separate empires met regularly but no one really knew who was in charge.

Our general point here is that in successful, aligned teams there is always clarity of leadership. It may be spread around, shared, or concentrated entirely on one powerful individual, but it's usually clear at any one moment who is doing the leading.

Loyalty to leadership

" He played the King as if afraid that somebody else would play the Ace! "

Kenneth Tynan, reviewing an actor as Richard III

In the theatre they say 'When you act the king, you only appear royal when those playing your subjects start relating to you as a king'. The message here is **it's other people who define you as a leader**. If a team doesn't relate to someone as their guiding spirit, it undermines the leadership. The killing may not be obvious, the absence of loyalty being entirely covert. For instance, moaning, whingeing, sniping and bitching are covert leadership killers when allowed to continue for long enough.

What happens in stage shows and performing groups? There's no lack of bitching, the theatre is famous for it. But most of it occurs after the show, rather than during it. Once committed to the task and the leadership, there tends to be 100 per cent effort by everyone, at least for an agreed period.

Many a potential stage flop has become a hit despite an abysmal director, weak script or only average music. Why? Because the cast decided they were fully committed to the leadership and making the show work. Better the mildly bad taste in the mouth of the director receiving unwarranted praise than the sourness of complete disaster.

We are not advocating blind loyalty to the leader. That doesn't work either: it led to the troubles at Brent Walker, the Guinness debacle, and the Robert Maxwell saga. Yet aligned teams wanting to give a star performance need to establish a resilient loyalty to their leadership.

George Davis, who founded the successful Next clothing company, had 8 good years running it. Yet in the ninth year, when things began to go wrong, he was removed by the board. There was no resilient loyalty and some believe the company has never recovered from the team's regicide. Davis lost his crown partly because he had no agreed time boundaries around his leadership. At the first real crisis, he fell. Teams need a chance to review their leadership; it helps everyone when team loyalty has a definite boundary.

Once you have agreed to participate in a project and accepted someone as leader for a fixed time scale – stick to your agreement!

Leaders - who needs them?

No one is indispensable – not even leaders. Some of the most successful performing arts teams have evolved good leadership without focusing all the responsibility on one person. They may once have relied on a powerful individual yet are now famous as an entity – not

Explore ways for the team's leadership to be debated and reviewed. Try using these two questions:

From the leader to the team:
'How can I make your job as a team easier and you more effective?'
From the team to the leader:
'How can we make your job as a leader easier and you more effective?'

An honest sharing of the answers can help strengthen the team's alignment and enhance loyalty to the leadership.

because of their leader, e.g. the Berliner Ensemble, the Royal Shakespeare Company, Steppenwolfe of Chicago, the Bolshoi Ballet, the National Theatre, the Moscow Arts Theatre, La Scala Milan, La Comédie Française, the Ballet Rambert, the Moscow State Circus, the Berlin Philharmonic, the Royal Court. The excellent Royal Exchange Theatre in Manchester had five artistic directors, the superb fringe Bush Theatre in London had three, and the famous improvization group Theatre Machine worked brilliantly as a co-operative.

It's often a shock for leaders to see how well the team performs without them. Yet this doesn't necessarily suggest they are redundant. In a television programme on the role of the conductor, André Previn wanted to show he was indispensable (in a tongue in cheek way). He started the orchestra off, then suddenly left the platform. The audience waited for the music to fall apart.

Instead the team functioned perfectly, completing the rendition with much aplomb. Previn used it to show the conductor's job was more subtle than merely getting the team to continue doing what it patently could already do. He was demonstrating that while technically the orchestra could happily play all the notes, what the conductor brought to the party was unique. He could help the team go beyond mere technical competence to create something special.

In business too some teams have made leadership work in unusual ways. The American manufacturing company W. L. Gore and Associates, which produces insulating materials for clothing, surgical implants and high-tech cabling, has no hierarchies or managers. Not even the chief executive has formal authority over another individual. The staff, called associates, gain the skill to lead through experience.

Gore's whole approach requires leaders to gain commitment and loyalty from other associates most appropriate to their needs. While there are no managers, there are team, area and business leaders. For over 30 years and with annual sales running at $500 million a year, the company has successfully relied on people following team leaders out of respect, not duty.

If there is to be a leader, make sure this person is aligned to the team and has something special to contribute; otherwise leaders just get in the way.

Responsibility: make space to question and clarify responsibility for leading and decisions .
Deadlines: set one for assessing the leader's work.
Measurement: develop ways to assess the achievement of the leader and reduce ambiguity about whether the job has been done or not.
Feedback: create mechanisms for the leader to receive feedback and ultimately criteria for deciding when a leader should no longer lead.

ACT ONE - Scene 1 "ONCE MORE UNTO THE BREACH" - Aligned Leadership

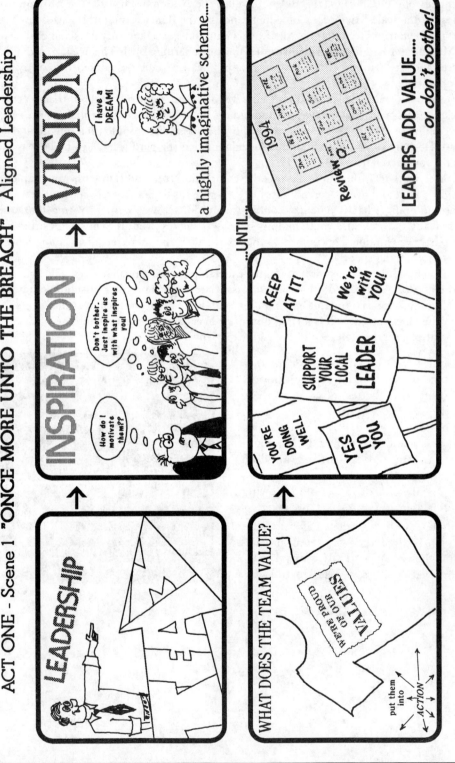

"Eighty per cent of a successful production is in the casting."

Lindsay Anderson

Scene 2 - **'WHOSE LINE IS IT ANYWAY?'**
Incisive Organization

Incisive Organization

Our theatre director pays a surprise call on the managing director.

MANAGING DIRECTOR:	*What are you doing here?*
THEATRE DIRECTOR:	*At least I know where to find you. How come we can never get to meet these days?*
MANAGING DIRECTOR:	*It's impossible. Disorganized chaos. I've been chasing myself all day. We may be aligned but at the moment what that means is – all the mess comes back to me. Still, I shouldn't go on about it, I'm sure you're used to all this manic disarray. What with all your prima donnas having tantrums and getting drunk all the time. Although I suspect you call it something arty-farty like . . . 'creative confusion'!*
THEATRE DIRECTOR:	*Quite the opposite. I can't bear disorganization. I find it impossible to give my best. And the truth is, artistic work demands stringent discipline. You look at Gillian Lynn choreographing a musical like* **Cats** *or Spielberg directing an elaborate scene with thousands of extras. Or even the discipline it takes for, say, Judi Dench or David Suchet to memorize one of the major Shakespearean roles.*
MANAGING DIRECTOR:	*Fair point. Maybe it's the other way round?*
THEATRE DIRECTOR:	*What d'you mean?*
MANAGING DIRECTOR:	*Well, maybe it's the arts that are well-organized and business that's in a state of chaos. I mean somebody's even written a bestseller about how to thrive on it!*
THEATRE DIRECTOR:	*I don't think we're paragons of virtue, but I think disorganization shows up more obviously in my line of work.*
MANAGING DIRECTOR:	*How do you mean?*
THEATRE DIRECTOR:	*Take the old story of a group of actors rehearsing, when someone forgot their words. The prompter whispered the missing line, but the actors were still stuck. So the prompter repeated it louder and louder, till eventually one of the actors snapped, 'We know*

	what the line is . . . but who is supposed to say it?'
MANAGING DIRECTOR:	*Oh, I see what you mean. When I go and see a show, every line follows another, everybody seems to know what they're doing – like clockwork. If two people overlapped, it would show up instantly.*
THEATRE DIRECTOR:	*Exactly. We simply can't function without a high degree of rigorous organization. That's why things are arranged the way they are – rigid time scales, distinct responsibilities . . .*
MANAGING DIRECTOR:	*And clear roles – knowing who does what.*
THEATRE DIRECTOR:	*Precisely. And one other thing.*
MANAGING DIRECTOR:	*What's that?*
THEATRE DIRECTOR:	*We tend to separate the administrative activity from the creative activity. It's hard to concentrate on the creative side when you're running around like headless chickens trying to organize things.*
MANAGING DIRECTOR:	*Ah, 'headless chickens', that reminds me . . . must dash!*

Casting

" Eighty per cent of a successful production is in the casting. "

Lindsay Anderson

Casting in the theatre is similar to a business team recruiting a new member. The artistic director wants to know that people joining the team have similar values, that they agree on the purpose and are equally committed. As if that's not enough, they're expected to bring a personal style and creative contribution to it all.

The job of the artistic director is to know if they will do what's required. It's not clairvoyance. Both performers and directors are skilled at spotting the person with the right flair to join their team. Performers are good at it because they spend much of their life being interviewed and auditioned for jobs. They are used to discussing approaches, negotiating interpretations and understanding a director's intentions. Directors are usually good at it because they get a lot of help, and it's partly why they are successful in the first place.

The agenda of talented stage directors in casting has some lessons for business teams too. They look for a person's **values, purpose, commitment and creative contribution**. This is exactly what ACE teams need to focus on when defining and refining their membership. Of course many business teams do not start from scratch, as happens when a director casts a new play. But increasingly in business many teams are temporary, set up for specific purposes and then disbanded.

As with business recruiting, casting for the theatre is often a highly professional process, using expert help. Take Doreen Jones, for instance. She has cast various Granada television programmes that need actors who resemble famous people, like the Prime Minister or Poland's Lech Walesa. She doesn't just read the script and pick a few names from a stage directory. As she explains, 'I get the director to talk to me a lot about the spirit of the character'. Through her work she becomes an extension of the Director's own instinctive selection talents. So casting in the theatre can be quick and efficient, simply by thoroughly understanding what one is seeking.

The most celebrated artistic search for the right team member was Selznick's hunt for Scarlett O'Hara in *Gone with the Wind*. It took 2½ years, during which talent scouts visited every hamlet in the American South. By the time Vivien Leigh finally appeared to read the few lines given her by director George Cukor, he had heard them hundreds of times from trained and untrained actresses of every shape, size and talent.

> When recruiting to build an **ACE** team, look specifically at:
>
> 1 Values.
> 2 Purpose.
> 3 Commitment.
> 4 Creative contribution.
>
> Try exploring these by reviewing with potential team members:
>
> - 'What really matters to you as a person, what do you most care about?' – their values.
> - 'Why are you here, why do you want to work with us, what do you most want to achieve for yourself if you join us' – their purpose.
> - 'Why does joining us matter to you and what will you do if you can't' - their commitment.
> - 'What could you offer our team that's new, or different or special' - creative contribution.

Why did he choose her? Because, as he said at the time, it was the first time he had been *moved* by those lines. Has this any implications for how business teams recruit? Well, Vivien Leigh was chosen because she was special. **The director knew immediately that this was the person who brought something unique to the team**. This is how you build ACE teams. You begin by making sure that the members bring something special, not pedestrian, to the team.

Of course business cannot make the sort of effort used in *Gone with the Wind*. If it did, most companies would go broke, although the cost charged by some corporate head-hunters these days make Selznick's costs almost look cheap. Nor can the film industry itself afford Selznick-style recruitment, apart from rare occasions. Which is why past performance matters a great deal and why another solution is to ask a few people to do screen tests. (Screen tests and auditions show people at work – actually performing.) Such tests are hardly relevant for business teams, yet they need something like them, instead of relying as heavily as they do on formal interviews.

Interviews alone are a sure way of failing to recruit the right ACE team member. Research has consistently shown the weakness of this method of finding people who will succeed. Selection in many companies tends to focus on selecting for the job, with far less attention on what a person might contribute beyond that. It's usually assumed if they can do the job well, that takes care of the team issue. Some companies do look carefully into whether someone can work well in a team. The point here is, there are more imaginative ways than just interviewing to discover whether it's the right person.

The musical world, for instance, shows that playing together is a fine way of making more sense of recruiting to an ACE team. Guest conductors may lead an orchestra on many occasions before finally being offered a full-time post. Actors may have parts in several plays with a company before being asked to join the repertory as permanent members.

It's a kind of probation, and business teams that can organize the equivalent also gain benefits. The main aim is to develop situations in which the team and the potential new member discover how they relate to each other: whether they would enjoy being together and can challenge each other creatively, and could develop their potential, and thus begin to produce star performance.

There are also systems that describe what kind of team member the person is likely to be, such as Belbin's famous research, which we mentioned earlier.

> Give potential recruits to a team the chance of 'playing together' with it:
>
> • Create opportunities for them to join the existing team, like spending a morning brainstorming with it or perhaps playing a business game.
> • Or go away with the potential new member and do something creative together, such as making a video. You soon discover how people work together under pressure.

This useful classification describes people's preferences for various team roles, such as chairman, ideas person or team worker, and indicates how they are likely to behave.

Labelling team membership in this way offers helpful insights, but it can also lead to tunnel vision. When ACE teams are really performing well, such classifications tend to break down as people grab all the roles, or ones that they never expected to play. Part of growing and developing as a human being is learning you can defy classifications and be what you never previously expected.

Objectives

" The trouble is Mr Goldwyn, that you are only interested in art, and I am only interested in money. "

George Bernard Shaw

Apart from building the right form of team membership, ACE teams also need to be closely aligned on objectives. Successful performing arts teams invest enormous energy making sure everyone is aligned on these. It is as important as in any business team. Otherwise orchestras don't play in time, chorus girls stumble out of step and actors fluff their lines.

ACE teams are:

- Exceptionally clear about their objectives.
- Exceptionally committed to them.

Objectives is a jargon word for the more detailed things a team wants to achieve. To escape the jargon trap let's consider Stanislavski.

'Stan who?', you may ask. He was a theatrical producer who influenced such names as Marlon Brando, Rod Steiger, James Dean, Meryl Streep and Robert De Niro. These names at least will be more familiar.

Stanislavski developed a system that was later adapted into the famous Method school of acting. The Method, sadly rather riddled with jargon too, is basically similar to life itself – it's easy to talk about and more complicated to actually do.

What is the Method about and has it anything to offer business? It says that all human beings do things because **they want something**. That is, every action we take is meant to achieve an objective.

When reading a play and interpreting a role, the actors' job is not merely to say the words and sound impressive. It's also to discover the characters' **objectives** – why are they doing what they do? Naturally they have changing objectives as the drama unfolds. So in the Method the actor uncovers lots of objectives. It can get confusing, which is why there will also be a **super-objective** – whatever the person wants overall. Like Robin Hood rescuing Maid Marion. The simple aim is to rescue her, the super-objective is to rob the rich and give to the poor. Hamlet's super-objective is to revenge his father's death; meanwhile he has many less grandiose objectives, such as setting up a play or talking to his father's ghost.

It's much the same in a business team. We may aim to win a big contract but our **super-objective** is to collar a bigger market share. Stanislavski also suggested interesting drama arose through obstacles getting in the way of objectives. It was the blocks that generated interest, because you've got to do something about them.

For instance, the sort of obstacles we face in the drama of *our* everyday business life are such things as difficulties in finding exciting training venues, a client's lack of training budget, competitors in our market, keeping our programmes fresh, logistics and the pressures of time. Tackling these problems keep us buzzing as a team. After all, when the blocks occur, people have to overcome them, by taking ACTION

" Every objective must carry in itself the germ of action. "

Stanislavski

How does all this relate to business? Well, to sum up so far, these ideas can apply to all teams. Any ACE team needs to discover:

- What is our super-objective?
- What are our other objectives?
- What are the actual or potential obstacles that might get in the way?
- What action can we take to overcome these obstacles?

Finding the answers can help a team become more effective. In answering the questions, you are forced to become clear about **why we are doing what we are doing**. This helps a team avoid irrelevancies, wasting time and losing sight of what the group is all about. It pushes them to see the bigger picture.

When television was first invented, it posed a huge threat to the movie business. Warner Brothers and MGM both started a war with television, bidding for stars, cutting prices, attacking the medium in the hope it would simply go away. They could not see television as having anything to do with their super-objective.

However, the entire film industry did not go downhill. Universal Studios for instance was smarter. It looked at the situation more creatively, asked questions along the lines of the ones above and concluded 'Maybe we're not just in the movie business, perhaps we're really in the entertainment industry'. It managed to focus on the super-objective and keep hold of the bigger picture, if you'll excuse the pun.

Universal started buying up TV companies and making its own programmes. It concluded that its particular super-objective implied 'if we can't beat them, let's join them'. Universal made huge profits by simply knowing 'what business it was in'.

The question 'What business are we in?' is asked quite often in companies too, though not nearly enough. It pays enormous dividends and contributes to increased team alignment.

Of course some companies did it long ago. Cosmetic firms have long since realized they are in the business of selling illusions, carmakers peddle freedom and independence, computer firms see themselves as selling power over information rather than just pushing hardware.

In the performing arts, which normally operate on tight margins and where the cost of failure is high, they have to be ruthless about clarifying the objectives, otherwise the consequences can be horrendous. Making a full length feature film, for instance, is so complex and costly that without a set of squeaky clean objectives it almost certainly won't arrive on time or budget. The making of the film *Heavens Gate* shows what happens when a team is unclear about its purpose and fails to get everyone aligned to realize it.

What happened at United Artists was that a talented director got totally out of control and his team failed to help. His super-objective was to bring the picture in on budget by an agreed date. Instead his own objective took over and cost went through the roof. Justifying this, he said, 'If you don't get it right, what's the point?' The point is he lost sight of '**Why are we doing what we're doing?**' and the team failed. You could say he was merely trying to realize his vision, being single-minded. In fact the team was not well aligned on objectives. Even the most experienced producers sent to stop the rot made no impact. By the time catastrophic bills forced a halt the entire film company was nearly bankrupt.

This sort of nightmare does not just happen to film companies of course. When Rolls-Royce went broke some years ago, it was mainly because the directors had lost sight of the objectives and failed to align the team around them. Development overheads spiralled through the roof, and while some of the board were focused on sales or profits, others were obsessed with the new way of making metal stronger by means of carbon fibres.

So how does a team align itself on objectives? Apart from paying attention to naming and describing the objectives, it also means ensuring everyone in the team understands exactly what they mean.

In one team we worked with the group had received a brief from its senior manager and everyone thought they understood what he wanted. Later when the team presented its work, he took an entirely different view of what was expected. That sort of conflict can wreck a team. It's like a group of actors playing *Romeo and Juliet* for laughs when what the audience wants is to cry.

In our regular development programmes with clients we find teams need to work hard at achieving a mutual understanding of objectives. Like interpreting a script or deciding how a character should be played, it's an emotionally draining process. People push each other to the limit, discovering their view of what should happen and how they feel about it. It sounds obvious, yet many teams never get around to doing it in depth.

Ask each team member to list on a single sheet of paper their understanding of each team objective. Pin the separate sheets on a wall and review how they differ:

- What are the similarities and differences?
- What are the implications of those differences that exist?
- What has to happen for the team to improve its alignment?

Emotion is one ingredient of objective-setting that business teams often deny themselves. The culture of management science, and a demand for facts rather than feelings, have made much objective-setting anodyne and sterile. What feelings are the team aiming for? If they achieve the objective, what emotions will be released? Greater passion in the process might make it more uncomfortable to handle, yet would greatly improve the chances of creating mutual understanding and commitment.

Commitment

What, *again*? Yes, we know we covered the issue of commitment when looking at values, but the same applies to objectives. Are people going to make them happen or not?

A British study in the late 1980s by the Industrial Society into the pitfalls encountered by firms implementing quality circles found that almost half the problems were caused by management resistance and lack of interest. In other words, quality circles had failed through lack of commitment.

It's the same in the performing arts. When a new work by a composer fails, it is often because the orchestra does not want to play it in the first place. Too much lip service is paid to the idea of commitment when what matters is **checking the degree of commitment**.

> " **As I grow older, I pay less attention to what men say. I just watch what they do.** "
>
> *Andrew Carnegie*

In the theatre people are pushed incredibly hard to demonstrate their commitment through the exhausting demands made on them. You simply could not work under the conditions some actors accept unless you were entirely committed. And usually the team's leader is the most committed of all and shows it. Unless people become really committed to the objectives and show it, you simply won't make them happen. So what should potential ACE teams do?

It's back to Stanislavski and discovering what obstacles lie in the way. A first step is asking people what would make them committed to the objectives. It may sound naive, yet when you combine it with the second step of being really prepared to listen, people will usually tell you whether they are committed to something or what they need in order to develop the necessary commitment.

Working with a board of directors of a small design company, for instance, we asked each individual to rate themselves in terms of how much satisfaction they currently obtained from their work. Several members scored themselves below five (out of ten) and we began exploring commitment. We asked each to say how committed they felt to the team's objectives and what it would take to increase their commitment. One revealed he was only partly committed because he felt strongly he had no financial stake in the company. This later led to an altered share option scheme. Another director revealed he was not fully committed because he hated administration and desperately wanted to return to using his previously effective design skills. Subsequently a restructuring occurred that altered his role and reduced the balance of administration to design work that he was being asked to do.

> " **Movie acting is not three hours a day, but nine hours that you have to be actually on your toes. Plus you dream about the role at night and think about it on waking.** "
>
> *Gérard Depardieu*

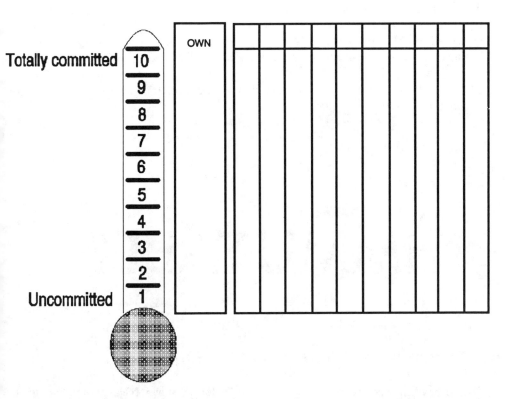

Totally committed — 10
Uncommitted — 1

OWN

Try giving each team member a copy of the **Commitment Barometer** shown above.

Mark your present degree of commitment to the team's main objectives. Be honest – it'll help in the long run.

Now in the grid on the right mark your own estimate of the degree of commitment of other members of your team.

Team members to share their own scores with the team.

Compare how people rated themselves with how team colleagues rated them in terms of commitment.

What will it take for each person to hot up their commitment status?

Summing up on commitment, we can say that as part of aligning a team behind its objectives it is always worth reviewing carefully people's individual commitment and discovering what might be getting in the way.

Time scales

Another alignment which an ACE team needs to organize is the time scale. Can you imagine the reaction of an audience to the following announcement by a theatre company:

Thanks for coming, the opening night's postponed for a couple of months. Please keep your tickets and we'll let you know the new date.

Yet this is how many business teams behave, always finding reasons for missing deadlines or not setting them in the first place.

In the theatre you hit deadlines everywhere. People seem to eat, sleep and breathe them. It hardly takes a real crisis to force action because someone is always inventing yet another inexorably approaching deadline. There are deadlines for the lighting plots, costume creation, set construction, programme copy date, technical and dress rehearsals. You name it, they have it.

Deadlines keep everyone on their toes. They keep galvanizing people into action, but only when the deadline is regarded as

IMMUTABLE

When deadlines are seen as readily movable, for whatever reason, their impact is always reduced. Tight, immutable deadlines stretch people to strive for the near impossible. Doing so, they discover new inner resources and more about themselves

When you face a real challenge backed by an agreed deadline that cannot be postponed, it has a miraculous power. Take one small instance. In an insurance company we were working with, a group of computer experts were making a video programme about their vision. They had made no perceptible progress for an hour. Time drifted, punctuated by arguments, desultory attempts to plan and back to more arguments. Told they had exactly 5 minutes left to begin filming and would have to do so whether or not they were ready, the response was immediate and explosive. Within moments the team had re-formed itself, made all the necessary decisions, and created a simple, but workable plan for achieving their objectives.

> **Ask the team to list its current deadlines:** _(suggestion)_
>
> - **Which ones are seen as immutable – 'ones we cannot let slip under any circumstances'?**
> - **Which ones are considered a movable feast? Can any be either eliminated or toughened to become immutable?**
> - **What happened to the last three deadlines the team set itself?**

Firm deadlines energize ingenuity, creativity and problem-solving abilities. People even forget to argue with each other or play politics. It pays to create chunks of teamwork, each possessing a clear deadline within which there is scope for people to swap around roles and inputs, to find new energy and then celebrate the completion of the work.

Like business, much theatre work is project-based. There are discrete activities, each with its own carefully designed boundary, which together make it possible to construct something as complex as a Broadway musical. Time scales are forced into the open and people readily accept them. When the Royal National Theatre, for instance, embarks on a production of *King Lear*, the whole team knows it has exactly 6 weeks and not a day longer to invent something exceptional.

A number of sales teams we've worked with find it hard to keep the enthusiasm and momentum going, particularly in tough times. Their task seems to be a never-ending slog. The advantage of project 'chunks' and deadlines is that the work is broken down into manageable parts. Each part has its energized beginnings and celebrated endings.

Stages of production

Let's look more closely at the various stages that occur in a theatrical production. They may not be exactly equivalent to what happens in a business team, but form a useful framework.

> 'Chunk' it. Divide the time scale into project chunks, with an opening and closing night. In between there will be other deadlines to keep the team's efforts in perspective.

First meeting of production and performance team

This is when everyone is introduced to each other and people discover to whom they need to relate for certain responsibilities. They chat and get to know one another. It's an opportunity for the director to outline his or her approach and vision.

The equivalent in business is when the team first agrees on what it is trying to do and what specific tasks have to be done to achieve it. Where business teams often seem weak is in hurrying over this stage of relating to each other.

The first read through of the script

Next the cast read through the play, normally with all the technical support team listening too. This is a crucial experience, especially when it's a new play never performed or heard aloud before.

Performers are nervous and keyed up; they are on the spot. Their colleagues are hearing them read and are looking for signs of interpretation. Directors take a definite approach to this task. Either they get everyone to relax and read it casually, or they build it up, creating a dramatic atmosphere a bit like a real performance. When they do that, like Walt Disney, they feel they're inspiring everyone in the work to be done. We recently heard of a director working on a Chekhov play who started with a Russian-style lunch, complete with samovars and vodka!

In business this stage is the equivalent of the first day's planning session for a project. The weakness here is a tendency not to consult all the eventual participants in the work sufficiently. There has been considerable pressure on business to improve its participative approach and this continues to meet some resistance. Participation is not always seen as desirable, with managers feeling it can affect their authority or reduce their power to make things happen. Yet the more you can bring those who can help into the discussion, the more likely the project will be a success.

The first rehearsal

This is the first time people actually get to their feet and start working properly together. Performers start relating to each other, and the director does his/her job while the stage management are working on the technical requirements. All except the person who's 'on the book'.

Traditionally, the person 'on the book' is a member of stage management who attends all rehearsals and records all the moves that the performers make. It includes working out where the sound and lighting cues will be, prompting the actors and preparing to run the entire show from the wings during the performance.

In business teams the first rehearsal is really when the group goes beyond planning and begins to get the tasks under way in a live work session of some kind. The equivalent to having someone 'on the book' is a project planner or an administrator who keeps track of everything. It really pays to have this role in a team that is facing a tight time scale. People can easily lose track of tasks and responsibilities in the maelstrom of the work. It avoids a lot of duplication and covering old ground.

First run-through

Now the team needs to take stock, and see how the whole show hangs together. There will have been run-throughs of each scene and act, but this is the first time people gain a sense of how long it will all take, what problems exist with the sets and costume changes and whether the characterizations are consistent. It's a tense time.

For business teams this is when deadlines begin to slip or arrive almost unexpectedly. There needs to be a regular space for formal review periods to keep projects on track and maintain the team's hold on the big picture.

Dress rehearsal

This is a first performance without the audience, although often staff from around the theatre watch. The dress rehearsal comes after a series of usually long and gruelling technical rehearsals. It has a climax all of its own, with an immutable deadline and nerves tightly stretched.

For business teams the equivalent of a dress rehearsal is when the team is almost ready for a major sales effort, a run-through for starting a new production line, a simulation day with pretend customers before opening a new retail store to the public, a practice for a major presentation, and so on. There are also fixed deadlines, or end points. The essence of the dress rehearsal is **testing whether you are going to meet the final deadline**.

First night

This is where the whole process has been leading, the opportunity to perform, to communicate the creative venture to strangers. Now the final ingredient of the creative process is added – the audience. This deadline is virtually always met – hence that famous expression 'It'll be all right on the night!'

The buzz backstage is amazing. The nerves, the excitement, hopes, apprehension, panic, energy, concentration and expectation all blend into a magical and powerful concoction. It's often preceded by the swopping of 'Good Luck' cards and presents, and perhaps followed by a party.

Business too has lots of opportunities for first nights. What it could usefully learn is how to inject more excitement into them, making them into something to celebrate.

The last night

Now it's the final performance, the end of the team's work together. Some of these deadlines are totally predictable, as when a show has a fixed period to run and everyone is aware of it. Others come almost unexpectedly, as when a show has done well but not well enough.

The final show is often a celebration, tinged with sadness and a sense of loss. If the whole venture has been a bad experience, there's a sense of relief. Sometimes it is marked by a party, emotional farewells and so on.

In business teams the closing deadlines are also quite variable, and there is usually rather less attention on how people feel about these endings. When people see a final ending being respected and feelings acknowledged, they feel valued and worth while. It makes them more willing to risk themselves and their commitment to the next major project or task. We will look at this more closely in Act Three Scene 3, 'Applause, Applause'.

Focused organization

How can a team be creative and produce a star performance when it's also worrying about irrelevant problems? Some ACE teams outperform rivals because they firmly resist becoming enmeshed in tasks that are not central to the main activity.

This is more than merely seeing the wood for the trees – it's more like separating the yolk and white of an egg. If you are worrying about basic administrative problems, you won't tackle the more challenging managerial issues effectively. We're referring here to how the team itself is organized. Is it incisive, has it separated the back-up it needs from the actual tasks it must do to perform at its best?

In researching two creative productions, for example, Professor Mangham of Bath University looked at the Welsh Opera's *Cunning Little Vixen* and the Bristol Old Vic's *Edward II*. He concluded that the administration was clearly seen as a support and not an interference. To foster the creativity of the teams he looked at, Mangham suggested there needed to be 'protection for the group'. As well as objectives and time limits, ACE teams need support staff to allow them to monitor their targets and to reduce other pressures.

The 1960s saw a wonderful productive team in Tony Garnett and director Ken Loach.

Together they created such memorable plays and films as *Cathy Come Home* and *Kes*. Tony Garnett's prime skill was said to be his ability to protect the director during filming from the daily worries of money and film stock.

Back-up allows the team to be creative. ACE teams thus need to organize their support so they are ready to produce. They must put in place a machine that works smoothly, allowing them to get on and perform to their full potential.

Take Siegfried and Roy, for example. They are magic super stars who earn millions of dollars a year doing stage illusions in Las Vegas. They are masters of the impossible and their shows are huge extravaganzas, complete with wild animals, dancing girls and spectacular high-tech effects. Every performance is a sell-out.

The shows are exciting and complicated. You have to be incisively organized to do magic on this scale. Roy himself says: 'Speed is our signature. Excitement, danger, razzle, dazzle and glamour have always been our way of doing things on stage and off'.

Behind all their sparkle and showbiz talks is an organization working to split-second timing and tight schedules. Even the animals must know where they have to be and when. To make it all happen, for the whole team to function like clockwork, there is a punishing schedule of meetings, practice and performance.

The magicians are doing the same show every night. Surely business teams are not like that? Well, what about sales teams that have to keep constantly giving the same message, an IT department that must consistently give a good service, or a factory team that must keep churning out the same product to the same standards day after day? Our message here is that ACE teams need to be highly organized in order to deliver. As well as alignment on team membership, objectives and time scales, and being incisively organized ACE teams also need alignment on roles.

Roles

Alignment on roles means that in a star performing team everyone knows why they are there and what they are expected to contribute. There is still scope to do the unexpected, it's just that ACE teams respect talent and direct it carefully.

Siegfried and Roy live on the outskirts of Las Vegas in a white Aztec dream house that the locals call the Jungle Palace. They share the 8-acre compound with their co-starring royal white tigers, supporting menagerie and numerous support staff. When the two magicians met, they developed their show by becoming highly organized and clarifying their respective roles. One took care of the magic, while the other concentrated on rearing and training the wild animals.

Yet roles need not be confining. Soon both magicians could play each other's role and they became a team in which the joins, like parts of their act, were invisible. While people can change roles in an ACE team, there is great respect for the specialist talent and a clarity about what role people are going to play.

Business teams also have specific roles and job titles. Yet these hardly tell you what someone will do when the team is actually working together on something. It's rather like in the theatre when an actor is occasionally given a contract for a particular role but with the rider '**To play as cast**'. This requires actors to play any parts thrown at them and further reveals the fact that the director is unclear about casting. The formula is normally a recipe for disaster. Vagueness leads to the actor expecting more than the director will offer, and by the time rehearsals begin, there's been great scope for misunderstanding and resentment.

It's what happens in business teams when, even though each person has specialist skills, they can contribute more to a particular project. There is a tendency to take for granted that because someone is called an accountant, for example, that solves the dilemma of what they will actually do when the real team work gets under way.

When teams are really performing at their best, all the formal roles may go out the window. This is both creative and right. Yet clarifying each person's expected contribution at the start of each new team effort is a way of becoming aligned on roles. Put more simply, it did not matter that Sarah Bernhardt once played Hamlet. What did matter was that everyone understood who was the prince, and who was playing the ghost.

Be clear – who is doing what? Job specifications are vital.

However, so many of these tend to be boring lists of conventional tasks that soon nobody ever reads.

Try writing inspiring, realistic and exciting job specifications. For example, consider including jobs such as:

- Debunker of pomposity.
- Ensurer that team has quiet time together.
- Cheer leader.
- Person allowed one wobbly a week.

ACT ONE - Scene 2 "WHOSE LINE IS IT ANYWAY?" - Incisive Organisation

TEAM MEMBERSHIP

To join, or not to join, that is the question?

LOOK FOR A PERSON'S......
Values, Purpose, Commitment, Creative contribution

SUPER OBJECTIVES

HOLY GRAIL

EXPANSION

CASH FLOW

RECESSION

MARKET IGNORANCE

COMPETITION

START HERE

OBSTACLES and *ACTION!*

COMMITMENT

Jump - or don't jump.
It's one or the other!

DEADLINES

OPENING NIGHT!
"ACE TEAMS"
First Performance
Tuesday 9th February

SUPPORTIVE ORGANISATION

KEEP OUT

Amazingly creative and productive team in the midst of concentrated work. PLEASE DO NOT DISTURB.

CLEAR ROLES

PROGRAMME
CAST LIST

MACBETH:
MACBETH:
LADY MACBETH:
MACDUFF:
THE WITCHES

DIRECTOR:
DESIGNER:
LIGHTIN'

"Treat people as if they were what they ought to be, and you help them to become what they are capable of being."

Goethe

Scene 3 - **'WHO CARES WINS!'**
Supportive Relationships

Supportive Relationships

The two directors meet in a park.

THEATRE DIRECTOR:	*How are the organizational problems going?*
MANAGING DIRECTOR:	*Solved. Look at this – time off!*
THEATRE DIRECTOR:	*Impressive.*
MANAGING DIRECTOR:	*Thank you. Yes, we're all functioning incredibly efficiently now. Everything is crystal clear. But, you know something, I wouldn't call them a team. They haven't gelled yet. They're all working separately. My old team were incredibly close. We knew each other inside out. On the other hand, maybe it's not that important. Who says everyone has to like each other. After all, if they're aligned, they'll get the job done. Perhaps it's too much expecting to enjoy the relationships as well.*
THEATRE DIRECTOR:	*I'm not sure it's about everybody having to like each other, but I do think that strong relationships get people to perform at their best, and really go beyond themselves. Sometimes they produce incredible results, just because of these relationships.*
MANAGING DIRECTOR:	*OK. Give me an example of something that would never have been achieved if it weren't for the relationships.*
THEATRE DIRECTOR:	*Here's one I heard about just recently. Did you by any chance see the film THE FOOL?*
MANAGING DIRECTOR:	*Must have missed it, what happened?*
THEATRE DIRECTOR:	*It was made by a husband and wife director and producer partnership, Christine Edzard and Richard Godwin. They had just had a hit with LITTLE DORRIT.*
MANAGING DIRECTOR:	*Oh yes, I saw that on TV.*
THEATRE DIRECTOR:	*Well, there was an important final party scene, and d'you know literally scores of famous actors, some of them from half way around the world, played all the tiny parts.*

MANAGING DIRECTOR:	*You mean there weren't any extras?*
THEATRE DIRECTOR:	*Not a single one. Someone at the time compared it to 'a huge cocktail party lasting all day, for several days'.*
MANAGING DIRECTOR:	*Sounds like everyone came for the booze.*
THEATRE DIRECTOR:	*No way. They came because of the relationships the Edzards had established on previous projects. People wanted to support them. Miriam Margolis, for example, only had one line. She devised it herself and flew from the West Coast of America just to deliver it. Derek Jacobi, who was in it, said 'Everyone's committed to Christine and Richard's bravery – they put their money where their mouths are. There's no frills like caravans, but everyone's made to feel part of the same working process. Christine takes endless trouble with everyone, even placing fresh flowers daily in every dressing room'.*
MANAGING DIRECTOR:	*Now I call that building relationships. In a way, that's what my old team were like. We'd do anything for each other. Mind you, we'd been together for years. I suppose that sort of thing takes time.*
THEATRE DIRECTOR:	*I'm sure your right, in the sense that relationships get deeper over time, but you know in the theatre the team has to gel instantly. We have to get very close, very fast.*
MANAGING DIRECTOR:	*Great. But how?*
THEATRE DIRECTOR:	*They need to communicate, care for one another, share their thoughts and feelings and respect each other. A bit like our relationship!*
MANAGING DIRECTOR:	*Oh, er, umm . . . Hmm!*
THEATRE DIRECTOR:	*You look embarrassed.*
MANAGING DIRECTOR:	*Well, we don't normally say that sort of thing in business, but yes, it didn't take us long, did it?*
THEATRE DIRECTOR:	*Exactly.*

" **Communication is and should be hellfire and sparks, as well as sweetness and light.** "

Aman Vivian Rakoff

Communication

How members of a team talk to each other soon shows whether the team is heading towards star performance. Among top performing arts teams communication is obsessional. Everyone wants to say how they feel about a performance and how it should be improved.

The other side of the talking coin is how team members listen to each other. Here we mean active listening, not passive silence by disinterested team members. To assess how well a team listens, try using the 'build on that' test. Here you monitor the extent to which members of a team during a meeting follow on after each other and build on the previous person's contribution.

Phrases like 'Yes but . . .' or 'What *I* want to say is . . .' soon reveal whether people are only half listening **while merely planning what to say themselves.** ACE teams build relationships because, in communicating:

- They tune in to each other's moods and wishes.
- They are aware of what is happening right now.
- They are honest with each other.
- They value openness.
- They leave space for the unexpected to happen.

SUGGESTION

To encourage a team to listen, try asking everyone who wants to speak to:

- First sum up what the previous speaker has said.
- Indicate whether their comments link to what the previous person has just said.

Have you ever put a vibrating tuning fork next to another one and watched the result? The second one begins vibrating too. An equivalent process happens with people.

Take for instance the spiritual and internationally famous community in Scotland called Findhorn. Apart from some extraordinary things that have happened there, such as growing giant vegetables in almost barren soil, Findhorn is renowned for its exploratory work in alternative ways of living.

What, you may wonder, has that got to do with business teams? Well, Findhorn is hot on alignment. Before any new activity occurs, the residents pause to 'attune'. There is always a moment of silence in which people let go of previous busy-ness and begin focusing on the current endeavour. It's a pause to let the team members tune in to each other and recharge their batteries – rather like a computer that needs to have certain items cleared from memory to free it up to handle a new task more efficiently.

Actors do it before a performance. About an hour or so before curtain up, the cast will often gather on-stage. They probably haven't seen each other all day, so they want to check in with their fellow team members and be together for a while. They may do voice exercises together, or physically limber up. This helps everyone tune in. They know they can't produce a star performance unless the relationships are strong. Business teams need to do the equivalent.

Tuning in, is not manipulative or intrusive, it merely implies getting on with people honestly and making space to do that, and valuing what others say. This builds relationships. To do this, a team needs to become aware of what is going on all the time.

Awareness of what is happening **right now** means reading what theatre people call the sub-text, or what the rest of us might call the hidden messages.

Such awareness tells a team who can do what jobs best, and how to motivate and release potential in others. It identifies those who are depressed and others who are frustrated or angry. This awareness is a marvellous tool for 'reading' the situation accurately. Once you know what is really happening in a team, it becomes easier to decide what action may be needed to move things on.

So how does a team develop this skill? In an ACE team everyone will gradually develop some personal ability to read the sub-text and be alert to what seems to be happening **right now**. Or it may be one or two individuals who are good at it. Whoever does it, it is not a passive process of merely watching or listening. You need to be fully there yourself.

By **being fully there yourself** we mean taking part, even if you say nothing. The result is heightened awareness of what is happening right now and being alert to:

- What is said; what is not said.
- How it is said and when.
- Who said it and why.
- What is done; what is not done.
- How individuals seem to be feeling.

Such alertness can be risky yet highly rewarding. Nor is it as difficult as it may seem. One of the authors once led a team of six managers who between them were responsible for over 1,000 staff. The senior group met regularly every Monday morning and began their session with a 'safety valve' – 5 minutes during which any member of the team could say what was making them angry or might get in the way of a successful communication session. At first the team balked at talking about their feelings in this way, yet after only a few sessions all the team members became willing to say what might be getting in the way. They developed considerable awareness of each other and what was happening in the room at that moment. It greatly improved communications and built the team.

What we are talking about also implies honesty. Actors, for instance, are used to being incredibly honest about each other's performance as they try out different ways of working. To outsiders such honesty can seem cruel or nasty, and occasionally it might be so. Generally, though, people recognize that honesty promotes high quality communication and ultimately effective performance.

It is easy to assume that because we have noticed how someone in a team is feeling, or understood what they are saying, nothing more really needs to happen. It does. There's a crucial stage missing. In teams it is not enough to 'imagine' a complaint, 'think' a compliment, 'feel' sympathy. Our awareness needs to be communicated aloud.

Try reviewing:

- How many times a day do I 'think' a complaint or a compliment, and not voice it? What would happen if I didn't stuff if away?
- Do I make it easy or hard for other people to tell me the truth?

Sammy Davis Jnr once thought an actor's performance in a film was outstanding. He was about to write him a note but stopped, assuming that he would already know how talented he was. The actor was James Dean, who died a week later. Davis always said afterwards he never again hesitated, always communicating how he felt instantly.

In our 1991 study of managers in seven major British companies, in which we explored to what extent these people were fully used at work, over half of them said their companies did not publicly reward or appreciate good work. Doubtless these companies paid well and eventually promoted successful managers. Yet still people felt their companies were not saying aloud what needed to be said openly and honestly.

> " Treat people as if they were what they ought to be, and you help them to become what they are capable of being. "
>
> Goethe

In ACE teams openness is valued by the group, and this implies being willing to cut across or find a way through traditional barriers of hierarchy and status that can stifle communication. We were working with a leading mapmaking company, and several key members of staff revealed how they felt totally inhibited in the presence of the directors. They became almost tongue-tied. In that case the solution was to develop their individual communication skills and to help them work assertively within their team to communicate more openly across the hierarchy.

Just as the seniority of the directors blocked communication in the mapmaking firm, theatre people joke about the minor star who needs two dressing rooms, one for himself and the other for his ego. Behind the joke is a recognition that people's self-importance can easily prevent openness. Equally a team's leader can begin creating a culture of openness that permeates the whole group, even an entire organization.

In Sedgwick Broking Services, for instance, the staff say if you don't want to eat lunch with the chief executive, never sit at a table for three. The CEO regularly wanders into the company's restaurant, joining any table with three people to find out what they are thinking. It's just one way to show he values openness.

The final element promoting good team communications is making space for the unexpected. By space we mean leaving room for people to use their potential in sometimes entirely unexpected ways. Putting it slightly differently, it is sometimes said people prefer listening to plays on the radio, because it has the best pictures. Radio leaves room for the audience to do the work, creating their own mental images in their imagination, creating the unexpected.

It is like a dancer, musician or actor being given time and freedom to work through tricky passages, to practise and explore them, without being leapt on by others demanding results. Making this space is the other side of what we know so well, which is talking and filling the void with what we have to say.

To help a team learn to communicate resentments try the 'two-week rule', which says: 'If something occurs in the team which you dislike it must be brought to the group by the next meeting, or within two weeks'.

If by then you have not voiced it, then you are obliged to forget it, without harbouring it as a grudge, regret or resentment. This simple idea can stop things festering.

By creating emptiness, you actually promote communication.

" If I start to become a star I'll lose contact with the normal guys I play best. "

Gene Hackman

You can see it happening in business when a leader knows how to delegate to the team members effectively. A person is asked to take on an extra responsibility, then given enough breathing space to find his/her own way of doing things. Or when a team has made proposals and leaves within them plenty of opportunities for other people to contribute creatively.

Caring

Teams also build relationships through caring. When a team is aligned, individual members will spontaneously give support to colleagues, without a senior person

When you delegate a task or responsibility to someone, think of it as giving an actor a new role to rehearse.
Give them a little time and space to practise it, so that they can find their own way of playing the role - before you expect to see the results.

SUGGESTION

organizing it. It happens when the team recognizes that every member matters. Everybody needs support.

Stage fright affects all theatre performers to some extent throughout their careers. Knowing that you're not alone and your fellow performers will care for you is one of the greatest gifts they can give you. Nor is it just performers. All the crew in a television or film studio, or people backstage in the theatre, show an incredible amount of concern. Many a performer has been nursed through nightmare performances by backstage 'troupers'.

When teams are taking risks, being creative, or facing strong pressure for results, group support really matters. How it happens may not always be obvious. The team may appear to be effortlessly coping with tricky situations, yet behind the scenes the members are taking care of each other, providing the kind of mutual support that enables the team to sustain itself. You may not have to sort out their problems; just saying

To encourage more caring and understanding in teams many companies now practise job-swopping or job-shadowing.
Somebody from accounts spends a day in engineering, or a person in systems goes on reception for a while. It produces a far greater understanding of other people's jobs and stresses. It allows team members to spot when another person is under pressure and to do something about it, or at least sympathize.
Organize job swops. (One company we worked with called it 'cross exposure' – Find your own creative name.)
Any exchange which increases team understanding is valuable.
In Shakespeare's time, on Twelfth Night, the lowest in the household was allowed to be 'Lord for a day'. How about someone else being team leader for a day?

SUGGESTION

'I know it's tough at the moment' could well be enough.

In summary, caring in ACE teams is not considered soft or weak. It's through caring that members show genuine concern for each other and enhance their communication skills. They keep at it all the time, never taking it for granted. In this way it steadily builds relationships.

Sharing

Relationships are also strengthened when team members do lots of sharing – merging ideas, pooling insights and not hoarding information. It is a bit like one of those lunch parties where every guest brings a dish. Somebody takes responsibility to supply the starter, others contribute a main course and somebody else makes the pudding. Everyone is responsible for the meal and shares the work. There is a group investment in the success of the meal – everybody owns it.

In quite a few teams you find people who talk of '*my* client', or '*my* contact'. Sources are jealously protected rather than shared. It happens because people are frightened that if they share, what they contribute will be stolen or lost for ever. It might even help a rival's promotion within the team.

It is understandable that people play their cards close to their chest when ideas and contacts are stolen or abused. Those who share are seen as naive or foolish. So how does one deal with this problem? If a team is to work productively together, you may have to

> In your team try sharing favourite pieces of music, art or books with each other; create social outings to each other's favourite interest; or go as a group somewhere completely different.

break a vicious circle of lack of trust . . . leading to no sharing . . . leading to lack of trust.

People may need to be helped to realize that only through sharing and pooling of ideas, information and insights can the team create something that is more than the sum of the parts. Certainly the shared lunch is more than just different people's dishes eaten in sequence.

To break into that vicious circle you have to be willing to work on the trust issue and begin to experiment with the benefits of sharing.

Feelings

ACE teams go beyond exchanging ideas or information. They also share thoughts and feelings. Perhaps this makes you feel slightly uncomfortable.

> If people keep talking about facts, ask them to speak about feelings; and when people constantly talk about feelings, ask them about the facts!

In business teams the focus is often on the task rather than what people are feeling.

Feelings may be messy, unpredictable and hard to understand, yet they can make or break a team. You cannot avoid dealing with them, and if you want to create an ACE team, feelings play an important part in its natural development. When these teams choose to share feelings, it is done constructively, not as a gossipy, pass-the-time-of-day activity.

Decisions for example, commonly go wrong when people fail to take notice of feelings – their own and other people's. Managers under-perform when feelings are banished to the apparent safety of out of work hours or to be dealt with by someone else, such as a personnel expert.

If a team is to reach peak performance and be creative, it must learn to handle strong feelings well. This is no time for 'stiff upper lips'. While strong feelings can be a destructive force, they are also a powerful energy source.

And it needn't take a long time. In our development courses we often start or end a session with each person expressing how they feel in one word. It takes a while for them to get more specific than just 'Fine' or 'OK'. However, they soon benefit from the practice and are able to be sensitive to their full range of feelings. At the end of it – each person knows the others' position.

> To promote more team openness, individual members need to share important personal experiences, share feelings as well as facts.
>
> Ask team members each to present an incident from their own experience – a turning point in their life, an event that had an impact on them. We regularly use this exercise in our Presentation Skills course. By the time people have shared aspects of their personal life that are important to them - the birth of a child, a successful project, the death of a loved one, a career move, falling in love – the members of the group always comment on how much closer they feel.
>
> It opens up conversation on a deeper level. Many groups complain that they've worked together for years and have never had this information. It fundamentally affects their relationships.
>
> *Warning:* Consider using a skilled facilitator who is used to helping teams develop this kind of sharing.

Many team leaders, though, prefer not to deal with feelings and focus instead on facts, the task and less unpredictable areas. Blocking the flow of feelings in this way can be extremely destructive. Team leaders who banish feelings from the group by, for example, quickly ending discussions, or who cannot show their own vulnerability, will never run an ACE team.

What then is the gain when a team is able to share feelings in the way suggested? The main benefit is you nearly always tap into a huge reservoir of energy waiting to be directed to more constructive ends. In our workshops, for example, you will regularly hear phrases such as 'I never knew you were so angry/annoyed/frustrated/unhappy/anxious/bitter/resentful' and so on. Until people have a chance to air their feelings, they are unlikely to move on to use the energy more constructively.

You see this happening after a company has been taken over. There is frequently an enormous amount of grieving for the old ways, or previous relationships, even if everyone knows that they were not the best. Until these feelings have been allowed to surface and are dealt with, newly created teams do not work at their best, or take far longer than necessary to reach full effectiveness.

Feelings of course are not only unreasonable, they cover a huge territory. Two of the strongest ones we've encountered that stop teams working well are insecurity and fear.

Insecurity

Teams that are steadily developing are continually handling uncertainty, ambiguity and the unknown. It's normal to feel insecure in such a situation – which is why ACE teams recognize that opportunities for mutual support must be created. People who joined banks and other so-called secure environments and were told they had a 'job for life' are now getting quite a shock, and may lack the internal resources to handle the feelings.

Creative artists have learned how to handle insecurity. Often they don't know where the next job is coming from, let alone whether the present one will be a success. Yet somehow they must continue and still do the job as best they can.

In business a successful team is also trying to achieve results, often exceptional ones. It has no guarantee of success. No wonder individual members sometimes feel lost, stuck, and unsure what to do next.

Part of handling insecurity is acknowledging that these feelings might be around and by bringing them into the open to deal with them. In short, ACE teams tackle insecurity in its members, they don't ignore it.

Fear

Often, though, in facing the unknown, teams are more than just insecure, they are positively frightened. There is fear of failure, humiliation, rejection, intimacy, discomfort, illness, mistakes – even success! In that situation surely what is needed is a tough manager – isn't it?

Sometimes a team's biggest problem is having a tough manager, who either does not personally have fear and believes others don't either, or considers the best way to handle fear is to pretend it doesn't exist. This style of 'macho-management', being positive and tough all the time, can become a tyranny. Even the toughest leaders and strongest teams need to make space for people to share their doubts, uncertainties and fears. You can often judge the quality of relationships by how much they can tolerate facing such difficulties.

Another way of putting the point we are making is Freud's argument that 'the penalty of resistance is repetition'. The more you deny and pretend something isn't there, the more it will haunt you.

Respect for the individual

> The founder of IBM was once in a lift when he spotted a casually dressed, bearded individual. 'Fire him!' demanded the founder, only to be told, 'We can't, he's your chief programmer'.

Respect is another of the building blocks of developing relationships in teams. What do we mean by that?

Well, let's take Beethoven's Piano Concerto Number Five, for instance. A much performed piece. It only sounds different because of the individual soloist's talent. To create a memorable product for the audience, he/she also needs the different and complementary skills of the cellist, conductor, piano-tuner and front of house manager. The point here is that to create something special demands respect for the individual. In ACE teams people are not expected to be the same. If they were, they would all be playing the same role or doing the same job.

In past years failure to wear a hat could get you sacked from the sales team, or a coloured shirt could brand you as unreliable. Yet there are still expectations of strong conformity in many places. Not always in clothing but in other important ways. What makes a team successful, though, is not conformity but diversity.

Spot the paradox? On the one hand, a good team depends on sharing values and being strongly aligned, but on the other a key value is individuality.

Often people's differences are considered a hindrance. You hear phrases such as: 'not one of us', 'doesn't quite fit in', 'hard to work with', and so on. Leaders who want to transform situations understand that people who are unusual – including the mavericks, the apparently awkward or hard to manage – often possess the real answers to what an organization should be doing. 'Tap the energy of the anarchist', argues Body Shop's Anita Roddick, 'and he'll be the one to push your company ahead'.

In theatre teams individual differences are relished. Take the role of Richard III for instance. Laurence Olivier, Richard Burton, Peter O'Toole, Anthony Sher, Ian McKellen, and many more have played it. What would be the point if they all simply did it the same way?

Or why should Nigel Kennedy make yet another recording of Vivaldi's 'Four Seasons' when Yehudi Menuhin has already done it brilliantly, using the same set of notes? He has done because at the time he believed his way of playing it would be different and therefore worth hearing.

To sum up, ACE teams work together for the greater good of all by making individuality a key value. Team members have a group commitment to releasing each other's individual self-expression.

> To help emphasize respect for differences in a team, ask each member to list on separate pieces of paper – one for each member of the group – the special contribution they consider that person makes, or could make to the team. Then:
>
> • One by one the members read out the list of attributes of an unnamed team member and the rest of the group have to guess who it is.
> • Or members read out what they have listed for a particular person and then present their paper with the attributes to that person as a 'gift'.

> **"Few things help an individual more than to place responsibility upon him and let him know that you trust him."**
>
> *Booker Washington*

Scene 4 - **'THE ANGEL FACTOR'**
Personal Investment

Personal Investment

> **" I don't care if it doesn't make a nickel. I just want every man, woman and child in America to see it. "**
>
> *Sam Goldwyn*

Our managing director pays the theatre director a visit . . .

MANAGING DIRECTOR:	*I've got a bone to pick with you!*
THEATRE DIRECTOR:	*Oh dear, I'm a vegetarian!*
MANAGING DIRECTOR:	*Hard luck, now listen. I've been reading some of those theatre books you gave me, doing a bit of research, and I want you to answer a question for me.*
THEATRE DIRECTOR:	*Fire away.*
MANAGING DIRECTOR:	*So far we've discussed team alignment in terms of leadership, organization and relationships. There's something vital missing.*
THEATRE DIRECTOR:	*I'm sure there is, but what do you have in mind?*
MANAGING DIRECTOR:	*Well take Laurence Olivier, for example. I read about when he was filming a scene in RICHARD III and an arrow was shot into his calf. Everyone went quiet while he sat there motionless, the blood gushing from his wound. When the assistant director rushed over to him, know what Olivier said?*
THEATRE DIRECTOR:	*'I'll sue you for this'?*
MANAGING DIRECTOR:	*Good try! No, he simply asked: 'Did we get it in the can?' He was so totally immersed in his work, not even being shot stopped him performing. So, what's the missing alignment factor – insanity?*
THEATRE DIRECTOR:	*Performers are a bit crazy, but I don't think that's it. You're dead right to pinpoint their commitment, though. Every time I watch dancers practise and see the gruelling physical torture they endure, I wonder what keeps them at it. And you know, the other day I was talking to an actor who worked with Daniel Day Lewis in the film where he played a paraplegic.*

MANAGING DIRECTOR:	MY LEFT FOOT. *He won an Oscar for that, didn't he?*
THEATRE DIRECTOR:	*Yes. Apparently, he stayed in his role when he wasn't filming. He literally lived the part. He wanted to experience what it was like only being able to communicate through his left foot.*
MANAGING DIRECTOR:	*So, what is it, dedication, obsession, screw loose, or what?*
THEATRE DIRECTOR:	*I think it's . . . personal investment.*
MANAGING DIRECTOR:	*You mean stocks and shares?*
THEATRE DIRECTOR:	*Not financial investment, something much more personal.*
MANAGING DIRECTOR:	*Such as?*
THEATRE DIRECTOR:	*Well, if you ask these people why they do it, they say it's not just a job, it's a way of life. ACE teams consist of people who are aligned about investing themselves totally in the work.*
MANAGING DIRECTOR:	*You mean a team of workaholics?*
THEATRE DIRECTOR:	*No, personal investment isn't necessarily about being workaholic. Take you and your team, for instance. Why are you doing it? What's in it for you? What's in it for them? You've got to look at what sparked your commitment in the first place. It could be the reputation of the company, the actual work, an opportunity to do something exciting, gaining a high profile. Maybe the project expresses a deeply held conviction; or allows you to stretch yourself for acquire some new responsibilities; or maybe you simply like the comradeship .*
MANAGING DIRECTOR:	*But somewhere along the line, you make a personal investment.*
THEATRE DIRECTOR:	*Right. And then people go to extraordinary lengths to create results.*

Investment

A good way of looking at personal investment is to notice what happens in mounting a stage show. The producer has to raise huge sums of money and it's usually a high risk venture. After all, there are many more failures than successes.

Even plays that receive much critical acclaim can lose money. Many films, for example, have won Oscars and yet failed at the box office. So obtaining a good return on your money from mounting a show is high risk, even if you happen to be Andrew Lloyd Webber. It's no wonder that investors who still go ahead and run these high risks are called angels.

" I don't work – I live! "

Gérard Depardieu

" I work to stay alive. "

Bette Davies

Why do angels do it? Usually they want to feel part of the action. When you invest your own money in any project, whether it's buying a house or backing a business, you now have a personal stake in success. You have a highly individual link with the final result.

An extreme example of this occurred when Alan Bowkett, a 41-year-old business school graduate whose career had spanned Lex Service Group and BET, became chief executive of food and property group Berisford International. He bought 6 million new shares and provided the company with £1 million in cash. As he put it at the time, 'I want to ensure that my objectives and my shareholders' objectives are the same. What benefits I get they get too'.

Stage performers of course rarely put their own money into shows, so why are they so committed? Their investment is more likely to be energy, enthusiasm, time, knowledge, passion, sweat and personal experience. Once you've put that sort of personal contribution into the kitty, you are bound to feel deeply committed. Which is yet another paradox. Without investing part of yourself, some part of you that really matters, you cannot make a real connection with a desired success. Yet if you don't have a strong feeling of being connected, it can be hard to find the personal resources to invest in the first place:

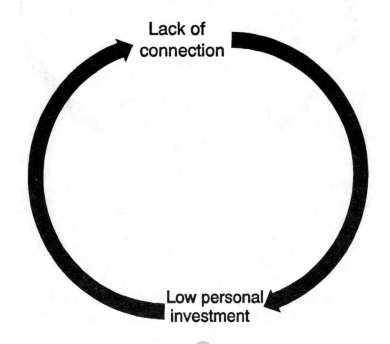

Lack of connection

Low personal investment

It's one more vicious circle that needs breaking into, if a team is to gain the sort of alignment we are talking about. So what breaks the circle? How do you persuade people to invest themselves so completely in the team's work that everyone becomes thoroughly aligned?

The way it's done is by helping people find the connection with their personal motivation and enthusiasm – let's call it the Angel Factor. It may not be a one-off piece of inspiration. It could be a whole series of factors that persuade us to invest so much of ourselves that it gives our team alignment a special edge. Factors such as reputation, the work itself, or a particular opportunity are all examples. Are there any studies or scientific evidence that make sense of these apparently hard to pin down intangibles. Well, a recent study by the psychology professor Mihaly Csikszentmihalyi at the University of Boston, for instance, looked at what makes human beings happy. He found that it is optimal experiences or 'flow' which give 'a sense of exhilaration that comes when you are so completely absorbed in a task that all your mental and physical abilities are being used to the utmost'.

What the evidence amounts to is that when people make a personal investment, the work becomes absolutely absorbing and highly satisfying:

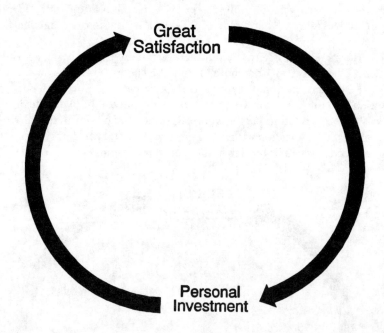

Living that kind of re-enforcing life is extremely demanding, but then nobody said being an ACE team is easy. To quote Siegfried and Roy again, Roy says:

> You have to be round the clock dedicated or it doesn't work. Our lives are really an extension of the show and vice versa. Everything we do – the people we see, the food we eat, the house we live in – relates to our performance on stage.

You needn't go *that* far, but we are talking about total immersion in the project at the time of doing it. The top teams in the performing arts adore their work and are totally committed to it. There is no holding back. People drive each other to new heights of achievement. John Goldman, the man behind the Monty Python films, for instance, had six writers constantly questioning each other about the standard and nature of the material they were creating. This mutually challenging process, Goldman says, made them better and better. No one could have forced these writers to suffer the agonies of constantly rewriting. They had to love it in the first place.

> **" My involvement goes deeper than acting or directing. I love every aspect of the creation of motion pictures and I guess I am committed to it for life. "**
>
> *Clint Eastwood*

In essence, team members passionately investing themselves in the group's work, or some important aspect of it, produces a powerful sense of alignment. The Angel factor encourages team members to make the connection between themselves and the objective.

> **" I'd rather direct. Any day. And twice on Sundays. "**
>
> *Steven Spielberg*

So let's look at some Angel factors at work.

Angel factors

Reputation

ACE teams develop a reputation that is magnetic. Performers leap at the chance of working with certain directors, conductors, choreographers or writers. There's a definite allure about being in the premiere of an Alan Aykbourn play, dancing a Kenneth Macmillan ballet, or singing with Placido Domingo in an opera – even if you are only in the chorus.

It's much the same in business. People want to work for certain companies such as Mars, or Hewlett Packard because of something special they offer. It certainly isn't the allure of profits or high turnover. There's even a directory now produced showing which companies are seen by people as the most desirable to join. None of the criteria have anything to do with how much money these organizations make.

It is not always national prestige that provides the Angel factor. Take the Welfare State Theatre Company, which galvanizes whole communities into creating epic theatrical processions, with huge puppets and pyrotechnical effects. The company's reputation precedes it and people clamour to be part of the fun. Success does indeed breed success.

Again the same occurs in business. Every industry has its top team known in the trade as the best, and to be invited to join is enough to set the blood racing.

The work

Another example of the Angel factor is the work itself. The opportunity to do what one does well can be enough to get the juices going and break into that vicious circle of lack of connection and low personal investment.

Two common reactions by performers offered a part in a new show are 'Good to get the creative juices working again' and 'As soon as I read it, I knew I had to do it'. Something about the new work – the quality of the writing, the message, the challenge, or whatever – creates the Angel factor, and people are excited to be part of it.

In addition, when you have a skill and do something well, you are usually looking for a chance to display it. For example, one of the authors used to appear in countless TV commercials – and it wasn't just for the money. Mini-dramas that have to tell their story in perhaps only 30 seconds demand a challenging level of technical expertise.

Composers who write incidental music for television dramas or films say how stretching it is to match the sound to the action. Ed Boyle, a former BBC reporter and now an independent producer, does radio work almost despite the money: 'Prices are rock-bottom and working for the radio is a loss leader. I really do it because I love the wireless'.

DISSENTING VOICE

" I've done commercials in Australia I'd pay you not to see – pretzels, fish fingers . . . "

John Cleese

Human beings generally delight in doing things well – like the enthusiastic carpenter we met who was working on a set of wardrobes. It was an old house and he was relishing the difficulty of coping with the crooked walls and uneven floors. Or like our own computer programmer having to devise a way of putting the ACE Team Star Profile on page 179 onto the computer screen.

Sadly, business teams seem to rely heavily on the assumption that the work itself is intrinsically attractive. This needs to be carefully checked out, particularly in senior management groups, for example, where the members may have long since drifted away from the roots of their original interest and expertise.

Opportunity

Another important Angel factor prompting personal investment is when people see an important opportunity for themselves. Theatre people say: 'There are no small parts, only small actors'. Countless players have moulded memorable performances from humble material. Stars such as Penelope Keith, Felicity Kendal, Michael Gambon and Tracy Ullman are often remembered for small supporting roles they played before they became famous.

In business one way people have tried to use opportunity as an Angel factor is through share participation, management buy-outs (such as NFC we mentioned earlier) and more recently the leveraged buy-out, like the one at Macy's in New York. The Macy's experiment ultimately failed through too much debt and insufficient growth. Even so, it showed the extraordinary impact of an exciting opportunity for personal investment in generating team alignment. Suddenly Macy's team began working together in a much more coherent way, because of the chance of personal wealth created by the buy-out.

> Teams and leaders always have choices about what work is done and how it is tackled. To increase the personal investment in the team through the work itself:
>
> - Ask what people like about the work, and think creatively about how they can have more of it.
> - Eliminate or reduce aspects of work that are not enjoyable, satisfying or challenging.
> - Help people discover for themselves how to connect the work with some important parts of their own life.

What this Angel factor amounts to is giving people a personal connection with a team's success. No job is too small or devoid of possibilities, it all depends on whether individuals see a personal link between themselves, that job and the team's success.

Which brings us back to the leaders. Their job is to ensure that every member of the team can make that link, and for those who find opportunity a compelling Angel factor, to help those people see it. When they do, they will make the necessary personal investment and contribute further to team alignment.

> To assess how far members of the team see meaningful opportunities for themselves in what the team is doing, have some fun playing the 'Opportunity Knocks' game.
>
> - Give each team member up to five blank cards. On each of the cards the member writes an opportunity or some successes potentially within reach of the team.
> - Collect all the cards and shuffle them.
> - A team member reads out what is on the card and the members give the item a score from one to ten to indicate how far it seems to connect personally with themselves in some way. Record the scores on a flip chart.
> - Items with a score below six are reviewed to see how they can be made more relevant to the individuals to strengthen their personal investment.

Innovation

Another way of encouraging people to make a personal investment and further team alignment is by using the attraction of being 'the first'. That is, when something is compelling simply because it is new.

Many stage performers, for example, are reluctant to participate in revivals, arguing 'What's the point of doing something that's already been done before?' And, in business, people are often more attracted to launching a new product than pushing the sales of an existing one, or setting up a new information system than refining the present one.

The allure of the new certainly seems to have a particular power. It persuaded celebrated actors at the National Theatre, for instance, to perform in drag, becoming the first modern-day, all-male production of *As You Like It*. It prompted Glenda Jackson to writhe on the floor demented in *Marat Sade* and Jim Dale to learn to walk the tightrope in Barnum. It led Helen Mirren and Ben Kingsley to give up everything in London to play in Peter Brook's experimental team in Paris.

There is something compelling about being in on the ground floor, of having a chance to grow and have a real influence.

> **" A wise man will make more opportunities than he will find. "**
>
> *Francis Bacon*

By reviewing regularly (SUGGESTION)

- what's new about this project, or activity,
- what it offers the individuals in the team,
- what areas of new ground we will be breaking,

a team can stimulate the individuals' connection with the project.

High profile

The chance of a high profile is an Angel factor that can really get people going. They will often invest an enormous amount of themselves because it will set them apart or in some way bring some form of public recognition. For every shrinking wallflower, there's a bunch of blooming roses waiting to be discovered!

> **" Passion for fame; a passion which is the instinct of all great souls. "**
>
> *Edmund Burke*

People will do extraordinary things to avoid the depersonalization our society seems to achieve both at work and in other spheres. They will pay large sums of money for car number plates that suggest their car is somehow different, or customize their front doors.

In organizations it can be attractive simply to have the chance to be seen, to gain public recognition. Joining a high performance group is an important way of achieving that, since an ACE team with a low profile is almost a contradiction in terms. Success inevitably makes it stand out in some way. People will be attracted by the glory of being part of a winning combination, despite the work pressures.

Conviction

One of the more complicated Angel factors is conviction – a person's deeply held belief in what he/she is doing.

Bob Geldof gave a year of his life to work on Live Aid. Jane Fonda made the *China*

Syndrome because of her personal concern about nuclear power. Kevin Costner took a huge risk making his debut as a director with *Dances with Wolves* because he felt so strongly about the way the native American Indians were treated.

Conviction is a powerful driving force. When people have it, they will often make an unbelievable personal investment and handle any consequences later. And they often do it without expecting much personal reward. The Women's Playhouse Trust, for instance, tries to improve women's lot in the theatre, and attracts actresses such as Glenda Jackson and Joan Plowright. Green Light Productions is a small theatre company committed to ecological improvement, and a percentage of its revenue is committed to an environmental cause.

Conviction can be more powerful even than profits. When Body Shop once again confounded the critics with its financial results in early 1992, a financial observer commented that earnings growth was way down the list of founder Roddick's list of priorities. 'If it came to what she saw as a moral crunch, Ms Roddick would probably sacrifice profits.' The thousands of staff working for Body Shop would only quarrel with the word 'probably'.

Nowadays there is a growing spirit of concern in business. There is the teaching of business ethics in management schools, and a number of companies participate in the Business in the Community campaign, and, most flamboyantly, in charity events. All are signs of people's desire to act out their beliefs.

The energy released when this particular Angel factor is at work is what every business yearns for. A basic question facing team leaders is how can the enthusiasm and vigour shown by staff in companies for events such as Comic Relief be used in their work too? These events are not always that exciting. There is, after all, nothing inherently thrilling about collecting money. The attraction comes from doing something one cares about, and having an enlivening experience.

One way is connecting with a good cause in your day-to-day work. IBM, for example, has long supported secondment of executives to provide specialist know-how and advice to voluntary organizations. Another way is using the company's resources to support particular local community needs. A third approach is tithing a percentage of profits or revenue to a specific cause. We ourselves, for instance, tithe 5 per cent of one of our courses to a children's charity.

Acceptance of responsibility

The next Angel factor is responsibility, which is when people believe it's up to *them* to create important team results.

When Beechams merged with Smith Klein and French, both companies were

> What causes in the world do individual members of the team really care deeply about?
> Find creative and worth-while ways of linking what the team does with those concerns. Such linkages can sometimes give team alignment a whole new meaning and driving force.

thought by many observers to be heading towards oblivion. Neither was big enough on its own to tackle their bigger multinational rivals. Morale in both companies was low. After the merger the new leadership began investing heavily in team development.

Over 100 top managers worked for months in groups that were given the most basic of responsibilities. In effect the top management said 'Forget about Beechams and forget about Smith Klein and French. Start with what we've got and tell us what needs to happen'.

> **" You can get people to develop their skills not by steering them by fixed rules but by giving them total responsibility to achieve a specified result. "**
>
> Jan Carlzon, Chief Executive of SAS Airlines

Although the exercise absorbed enormous quantities of management time, the team-building and shift of responsibility worked. When we met a relatively junior research and development supervisor in the newly merged company, he could not stop talking about the process that had switched on people's sense of ownership: 'It has filtered right down, and now more and more employees are being infected'.

Our message about this particular way of enlisting personal investment is that it can be encouraged by the members of the team feeling personally responsible in some way for an important aspect of the team's work.

> **" Few things help an individual more than to place responsibility upon him and let him know that you trust him. "**
>
> Booker Washington

> **SUGGESTION**
>
> Teams are a great way of avoiding anyone having responsibility for anything significant.
>
> Break down all team activity into significant and discrete chunks, with a specific person's name publicly attached to each chunk.

Ensemble playing

We've mentioned the paradox of needing to reconcile great individuality with strong teamwork. You can see this reconciliation occurring in a group such as the Ambache Chamber Orchestra. This relatively new team of musicians has a soloist and lead violinist, yet plays without a conductor. Their strength lies in the ensemble playing – the sense in which everyone is in it together.

This might seem true for all teams. Yet some teams mainly consist of strong individuals whose wish is to stand out from the crowd. There are also ACE teams, though, which shine by committing themselves to group success, and no one tries to stand out singly. It provides a great sense of companionship, community and friendship.

There are teams like this in business too, although companionship, community and friendship may not be at the forefront of their thinking. They are more likely to talk about wanting to work together because they value how effective they can be as a team or how they all get on with each other.

Few people join ACE teams solely for companionship or friendship, yet these remain important factors in most teams. For example, most of the research on why people resist change in organizations suggests how much they value their current set of relationships

> **" No rewards are handed out for co-operating with people we like. It's co-operating with stinkers that counts. "**
>
> *J. C. Penny*

If there is a history of difficulties around the issue of leadership in the group, it might be worth restructuring and redefining the team as an **ENSEMBLE**. Simply seeing it in that way might allow individuals to invest themselves more fully in the team's activities.

and don't want them altered or damaged. This concern also prompts people to stay in an organization. It even explains why people occasionally leave organizations only to return a few months later, wanting to get back to the team.

Leadership, organization and personal relations are the bedrock of alignment. Personal investment provides that extra contribution which makes ACE teams truly an alignment of angels!

ACT ONE - Scene 4 "THE ANGEL FACTOR" - Personal Investment

HOW TO CONNECT?

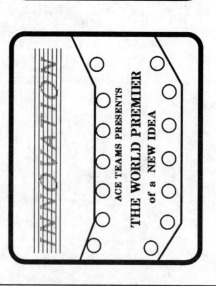

Act Two:
CREATIVE

Act Two: **CREATIVE**
PROLOGUE

PROLOGUE

" The best way to predict the future is to invent it. "

Alan Kay, Fellow of Apple Computers

Star performing teams are in the business of creativity. They innovate, take their creative ideas and apply them. It's how these dynamic teams renew themselves, stay healthy and produce outstanding results.

When people talk about creativity they often mean inventing ideas, rather than how to achieve exceptional results. Instead of simple idea-generation, ACE teams use creativity in its broadest sense to drive all their activity. Thus ACE teams keep trying to make everything they do creative in some way – from decisions to relationships, from plans to negotiating.

Since creativity can be hard to pin down, how do we really know a team is being creative? Take relationships, for example. It's rather easier to identify a group generating ideas than it is to notice a creative conversation taking place. Perhaps the best guide for what is really happening, and whether we're having a creative experience, is the feelings we have. For instance, do we end a meeting or finish a conversation feeling excited because something new came from the encounter, or do we leave frustrated because it was a turgid exchange of old information?

Naturally we see performers and stage artists as creative. But are business people? Well, since to *create* is 'to make or originate something new', there is no doubt that many businesses are amazingly creative. Yet there persists a myth that only a few people can, or even need be, creative, while the rest of us should concentrate on being productive.

We ran a team development programme with a group of project managers in the systems division of a large financial services company. On the last day we asked the group what they had discovered during the course. One of them said, 'I'd always thought of myself as an uncreative person. My wife paints, my daughter sings. They see me as a pretty straightforward computer bod. In these past couple of days I can really see how creative I am. I have ideas, I join in the devising process, I've been really active in all that we've produced. I now realize that I'm highly creative, it just doesn't fit the normal picture'.

In fact, when a team is being highly creative, concentrated and expressive, it's also at its most productive. While alignment is essential for star performance, it's only a start. There has to be a creative dimension too.

By now there ought to be some undisputed rules for what makes a business team creative in the broadest sense. Yet despite a considerable body of research, little is really known about the actual process and the mental mechanisms for controlling it.

The increasing diversity of companies is also changing the requirements of teams. Previously the emphasis was almost solely on sound management, now it's inspiring leadership that's wanted. And whereas in the past managers were expected to motivate their people, it's now quite rightly expected to be an empowering partnership. With these two changes, creativity is taking a more central role in teamwork.

> " Be brave enough to live life creatively. The creative is where no one else has ever been. You have to leave the city of your comfort, and go into the wilderness of your intuition. You can't get there by bus, only by hard work and risk and by not quite knowing what you are doing. What you'll discover will be wonderful. What you'll discover will be yourself. "
>
> Alan Alda – star of MASH

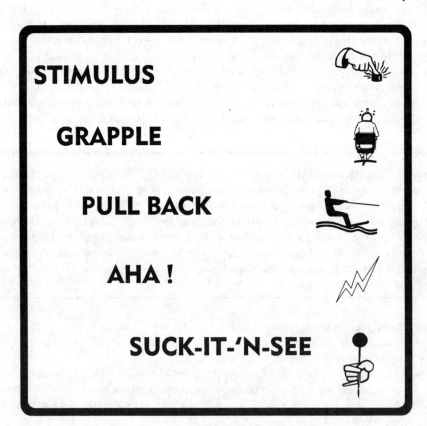

STIMULUS

GRAPPLE

PULL BACK

AHA !

SUCK-IT-'N-SEE

Before we show how an ACE team fosters creativity, let us see what the creative process itself looks like. While there are no agreed rules, there are common stages in all creative activity, although one may not always have much control over them.

STIMULUS: gets things moving. It may be imposed, such as a commission for a painting or a new symphony, the deadline of a production, or impending bankruptcy forcing a company to create a new product or solution. While there's nothing like a crisis to force creativity, this is essentially a reactive approach.

More satisfying and indeed satisfactory is stimulus that is self-generated, as when people follow their curiosity, or experience some dissatisfaction about the world around them. Like inventors, creative people are always looking and wondering. 'What's needed around here?' 'What would take this organization to a new level of effectiveness?' 'What else could we be doing to improve things?' They keep trying to see the world in different and maybe strange ways.

You don't need to be an artist to have this attitude. When young Michael Dell began selling computers direct to customers, without dealers, showrooms or using retail outlets, the idea was strange, and to many people at the time quite bizarre. Today, the multinational Dell Corporation is not so much strange as a model to be emulated.

To stimulate a team's creativity in the broadest sense, you may need to bombard it with new experiences.

We often get teams to commit to a 'new experience' or event every month, whether it be a ride in a hot-air balloon, or a visit to a rock concert, the Stock Exchange, an old people's home, a television studio, or a nursery school. It's always useful if the team members can pursue these experiences together.

What may seem an offbeat, strange or even irrelevant activity has a persistent habit of generating new team thinking.

Sometimes the stimulus cannot come from outside. The artist or writer always faces the blank page, even with a pile of existing ideas and materials to draw upon. The service department wondering how to produce exceptional customer care similarly faces a blank sheet. It's a common nightmare, resolved through the simple expedient of making a start, no matter how small. A painting begins with a single line, a play with a word. Once you've done something – *anything* – it often provides the stimulus to further work.

> **" I used to think that anyone doing anything weird was weird. I suddenly realized that anyone doing anything weird wasn't weird at all and it was the people saying they were weird that were weird. "**
>
> *Paul McCartney of The Beatles*

Making a start, though, does demand trust. It's like being at a planning meeting that begins with an eerie period of inactivity and silence. People need to believe that something will happen if they continue focusing on the issues at hand. From emptiness emerges the first contribution, which stimulates the next and so on. But no matter how good the stimulus, you still have to GRAPPLE.

GRAPPLE: an odd word to convey the striving, trying, organizing, frustration, playfulness, sorting, restructuring, hard graft, agony, release, struggle and persistence that is part of the development process. It's what the renowned psychologist Dr Rollo May once called 'an intense encounter with the material'.

All problems, other than the most easily solved ones, must be grappled with. You need to think about them, see them from different points of view, break them down into component parts, and so on.

"Genius is 10 per cent inspiration and 90 per cent perspiration."

Albert Einstein

By 'living with' the material for a while, one slides under its skin, coming to understand it from all angles. Scientists are used to such painstaking work, as are performers. It's tough and many of us prefer to avoid it. Yet there is no easy way round it.

"It's interesting isn't it – the harder I practice, the luckier I get."

Gary Player

After all this hard work you need to PULL BACK.

PULL BACK: the conventional way of showing a dramatic encounter in a film is through a wide shot, establishing the scene before moving into close-ups. Occasionally it's done the other way around. From a close-up you 'pull back' to show the bigger picture, which often reveals some surprises.

Similarly, in all creative endeavour there's a time to pull back for a different point of view, allowing another part of you to go to work. Your 'right brain' has to be engaged in the process, viewing things from another perspective, perhaps being quirky and unconventional. That can happen, for instance, through using symbols, drawings, metaphors, dreams, imagination – such as visualizing someone else solving the problem – and many other 'right brain' activities. What is interesting about this method, incidentally, is that it is enormous fun, which is so often absent from teamwork.

Creativity is sometimes about uncovering what is already there. Michelangelo even said his sculptures were already inside the blocks of stone; he merely chipped away the surplus material. Fax machines had existed in the Xerox laboratories for about 10 years before taking the market by storm. Left and right feet have been with us for millennia, yet left and right shoes were not made until the last century. Our assumptions tend to limit our ability to see what is staring us in the face – or at least in the foot!

Without an acceptance of the PULL BACK period, we can feel as if we're doing nothing, despite looming deadlines. Apparent inactivity is often really the gestation period when the seed planted in the unconscious stirs, begins to bear fruit. Leave it alone, sleep on it, go on holiday, walk the dog, do something else. Agatha Christie found 'the best time for planning a book is while you're doing the dishes'.

AHA!: the wonderful moment when something new comes into existence. An image, a story, a solution, a breakthrough. Anton Bruckner was once asked: 'Maestro, how, when and where did you think of the divine motif of your Ninth Symphony?' He replied, 'Well, it's like this. I walked up the Kahlenerg, and when it got hot and I became hungry, I sat down by a little brook and unpacked my Swiss cheese. And just as I open the greasy paper, that darn tune pops into my head!'

Archimedes shouted 'Eureka', and everyone has their own way of celebrating that satisfying feeling when you've cracked it. One may as well enjoy this moment, because now there is even more to do. You must SUCK-IT-'N-SEE

SUCK-IT-'N-SEE – if what is created will work. Testing allows refinement. A good TV script is redrafted at least four times. Most plays are rewritten during the rehearsal process, when the playwright, hearing the words come to life, gains fresh insight. The same is true in manufacturing, as a new product is improved during the production process.

It's tough work and hard to keep changing anything you have created when the strong AHA! experience leaves you wanting to end there. Instead it's crucial to keep going. You have to keep giving your best shot.

> **" The creative process is the flip side of the destructive one. If we are not funding the creative process, we are releasing the destructive process. "**
>
> *Annie Castledine – Theatre Director*

Based on the above process we suggest a creative team will encourage or allow:

- Experiment.
- Trust.
- Disagreement.
- Failure.
- Testing.
- Shared feelings.
- Play and fun.
- Using whole person.

We explore these in Act Two:

SCENE 1 'START WITH "YES" ' – Permissive encouragement
SCENE 2 'RIDING THE ROLLER COASTER' – Creative energy
SCENE 3 'MORE THAN THE SUM OF THE PARTS' – Using the whole person

> **"If new ideas are constantly turned down, it turns people off, they stop generating ideas, no matter how much you pay them."**
>
> *Anita Roddick*

Scene 1 - **'START WITH "YES"'**
Permissive Encouragement

Permissive Encouragement

The theatre director sits waiting, reading a business magazine; the managing director zooms in like a whirling dervish . . .

MANAGING DIRECTOR:	*Wow, we're really motoring now!*
THEATRE DIRECTOR:	*Great. I'm very pleased.*
MANAGING DIRECTOR:	*We're all aligned as a team, but something amazing is happening now.*
THEATRE DIRECTOR:	**What?**
MANAGING DIRECTOR:	*Ideas, suggestions, recommendations. I mean, I've always wanted proactive people with initiative, but there's no stopping them. They're coming at me with creative ideas left right and centre.*
THEATRE DIRECTOR:	*To which you reply?*
MANAGING DIRECTOR:	*Pardon?*
THEATRE DIRECTOR:	*Is that what you really say, 'Pardon?'*
MANAGING DIRECTOR:	*Come to think of it, I probably do say something like 'Pardon'. I'd like to be more positive, but to be honest, most of the ideas are rubbish – well, unrealistic anyway.*
THEATRE DIRECTOR:	*You remind me of a bank.*
MANAGING DIRECTOR:	*What d'you mean?*
THEATRE DIRECTOR:	*Well, it likes to say 'yes', but rarely does!*
MANAGING DIRECTOR:	*Point taken. But what about you, do you say 'yes' all the time?*
THEATRE DIRECTOR:	*When I'm rehearsing a play, everybody's suggesting ideas all the time. I invariably say, 'Let's try them out and see if they work'. If they don't work, those who suggested them are the first people to move on and invent something better.*
MANAGING DIRECTOR:	*Come to think of it, I remember working for a manager who always said 'no'.*

THEATRE DIRECTOR:	*And what happened?*
MANAGING DIRECTOR:	*After a while, I just stopped suggesting improvements. I felt completely uncreative.*
THEATRE DIRECTOR:	*The power of the word 'yes' is out of all proportion to its size. I tell you, there used to be a small theatre group that provided a whole evening's entertainment based on the notion of starting with 'yes'. One of them would walk on to an empty stage and start exploring an idea. It might be a character, a word, a hat, a physical shape – or a suggestion from the audience.*
MANAGING DIRECTOR:	*A bit like that TV improvisation show where the audience contributes ideas and the actors have to make a funny sketch out of them?*
THEATRE DIRECTOR:	*Right. Whatever the idea, the members of the cast always say 'yes' to it. There's no judging, no request to the person to alter the suggestion. It doesn't always work, but the outcome is spontaneous, interesting and often brilliant. In our business and yours, the killer of creative potential is 'no'.*
MANAGING DIRECTOR:	*Well I agree that 'yes' is a powerful concept. But why particularly for fast team-building?*
THEATRE DIRECTOR:	*When a team culture is all about 'yes', it encourages people to be creative by giving them permission. And not just permission to be right all the time.*
MANAGING DIRECTOR:	*What else then?*
THEATRE DIRECTOR:	*I'd say permission to experiment, disagree and to make a few mistakes.*
MANAGING DIRECTOR:	*Well, we've all made a few of those.*

Need for encouragement

" I'm not afraid to fail, providing I fail honourably. "

David Putnam

We once advised in a company where the finance director was nicknamed 'Doctor No' by his colleagues. As you can imagine, the atmosphere was depressing. It was impossible to convince him about anything. It was causing growing problems because people wouldn't go to him with suggestions, they already knew the answer.

Having identified the problem, we began exploring why he always seemed so negative. It turned out he had legitimate concerns about the profitability and security of the company. He was genuinely fearful about letting go, of saying 'yes', in case people went wild. Once he himself realized what was happening and that most ideas coming forward were not bound to end in terminal failure, he began tempering his financial caution with a more receptive attitude.

" If new ideas are constantly turned down, it turns people off, they stop generating ideas, no matter how much you pay them. "

Anita Roddick

We'll return later to the idea of terminal failure. Essentially, though, teams must distinguish between actions that could be merely damaging to the organization and those that might cause its demise. The restrictive climate is often imposed on individuals and teams by organizations because, like Doctor No, they confuse terminal failure with mistakes. The latter are inevitable along the way to discovering how to succeed. Discovering how to succeed, means developing a team climate in which suggestions are likely to meet an initial 'yes'. When that occurs, people keep returning with more. Even if your idea ultimately receives a 'no', at least you feel you're being taken seriously.

New business ideas, in fact new businesses, start with 'yes'. While generating ideas is valuable, it's saying 'yes' and acting on them that really matters. It brings a positive drive, a creative spirit to a team.

Conducting their interviews at 3M, *In Search of Excellence* authors Peters and Waterman were surprised that proposals for a new product rarely exceeded five pages. A vice-president explained: 'We consider a coherent sentence to be an acceptable first draft for a new-product plan'.

While running for the top job in the ailing Disney Corporation, Michael Eisner learned he might not be appointed after all. Ringing Sid Bass, the company's major shareholder, in Fort Worth, Eisner explained why he should be chosen:

It's going to take a creative person to run this company. Look at the history of America's companies. They have always gotten into trouble when the creative people are replaced by the managers.

Creative people start with 'yes' – and business needs them. When an organization reaches a certain size, though, it often starts having trouble coping with both releasing and harnessing creative flair. Instead increasing effort and resources are devoted to systemizing, standardizing, and homogenizing. While these are essential if an organization is to continue developing and avoid terminal failure, they have to be strongly counterbalanced by the 'yes' mentality. Otherwise they drive out the creative, entrepreneurial flair that makes growth possible.

This balance of form and flair is needed in a team just as much as in the organization at large. But how do you achieve such a balance? By helping individuals, teams and companies rediscover the joy and usefulness of ceativity.

It is tempting to lay this responsibility entirely at the door of the team leader. Yet ACE teams don't necessarily require their leaders to be exceptionally creative themselves, though that certainly helps. It's more important that there is a process of continual encouragement to release the group's creative potential.

> ## " You know how I'm smart? I've got people around me who know more than I do. "
>
> *Louis B. Mayer*

It's up to the whole team to generate and maintain that kind of encouragement. Expecting only the leader to do it is like demanding the leader do everyone's job. Everybody has the responsibility in an ACE team to avoid stifling creative possibilities by opposing restrictive practices. We're not talking about union rules or go-slows. Creativity in a team is choked off by:

- Routine.
- Hierarchies.
- Power struggles.
- Cynicism.
- Negativity.
- Disempowerment.
- Buck-passing.

> ## " I have a very low regard for cynics. I think it's the beginning of dying. "
>
> *Robert Redford*

During our team development work in companies we often meet staff who feel restricted and imprisoned by their working environment. What's needed is simply a more receptive and ultimately creative culture, one which starts with a 'yes' attitude. When an organization moves in that direction, then routine, hierarchies, cynicism and so on become less dominant. People soon reveal how liberated, powerful and productive they feel.

> ## " Do not be too timid and squeamish about your actions. All life is an experiment. "
>
> *Emerson*

Permission to experiment

As we heard from our theatre director at the start of this scene, one of the commonest expressions in all creative endeavour is 'let's try it'. The continuous quest for a workable idea demands experiment. Creating something new always requires a move beyond familiar territory. In a creative team you regularly suspend old ways of judging ideas, and challenge conventional wisdom.

When Edison did his countless experiments to produce a light bulb that lasted, he didn't decide beforehand which type of filament would work. The only way to tell was by trying out thousands of them.

Instead of 'Yes, let's try it' in many teams you hear phrases like 'I don't think that'll work', 'We've done something like that in the past' or, most frequently, 'Yes, *but* . . .'

> Do a YES/NO audit on yourself, the team or even the company: *(SUGGESTION)*
>
> - Notice how many times a day you say each word, especially 'Yes but . . .'
> - What would you expect other people's instinctive reaction to be to you, 'yes', or 'no'?
> - What about the team? Are you seen as a team that starts with a 'yes' or a 'no'?

Of course people need to be free to disagree, to show they don't approve of something; they can't always keep saying yes. We'll deal with that in a moment. What matters, though, is having a team climate in which 'yes' is the norm, in which 'Let's try it' is a way of life. The potential of teams and companies is locked away in the people who work there and who feel they do not have permission to contribute. When asked why they don't speak up, a common reply is 'What's the point. No one listens'.

So listening means saying 'yes'. You keep saying it so that ideas move forward until, if necessary, they hit some immovable brick wall. That's why a culture that says 'Let's try it' is so invigorating.

Who provides the brick wall – the Doctor No we mentioned earlier? No. In a team living by a creed of 'Let's try it', not every idea is pursued. That would obviously be impossible. 'Let's try it' simply liberates everyone to think creatively about what would happen if the idea was put into action. Quite often genuine obstacles soon emerge naturally to make it clear the idea is unworkable or not a priority. Living by 'let's try it' explains the success of certain Japanese companies one of which regularly reminds employees: **'You are not paid to come to work, you are paid to improve the business.'**

" . . . by chance you will say, but chance only favours the mind which is prepared. **"**

Louis Pasteur

The passion of theatre and other performing teams to encourage experiments is why many of them build so fast. Stage director Stephen Berkoff describes an atmosphere in which 'everyone experiments together. Ideas are thrown around, things are tried out, there's a buzz of concentrated creative energy. I want people to be desperate to get out of bed and go to rehearsal'.

Berkoff's world demands this experimental culture, but does business? The good ones that grow do. All the concern about total quality management, quality circles, just-in-time and a host of other catechisms of modern management is really about ways of encouraging everyone to keep pushing forward with new, creative solutions to run the business better.

It's peculiar that many business successes seem to happen almost despite the ability of the organization to say 'no'. One of the most memorable examples was the creation of the IBM 360 computer, which was never regarded by the company's management as mainstream. The company's development funds were channelled to an entirely different team, which was expected to make the product breakthrough.

The team creating the 360 was barely tolerated and was not even known to exist by some senior IBM staff. It had to beg, borrow and filch the resources for its brainchild. When the mainstream IBM project turned into a disaster, the 360 emerged from the shadows as a company saviour. It was success through the backdoor. Today this backdoor way of saying TRY IT – where teams are expected to skulk in the shadows – even has a formal name: skunk works. People talk of wanting more skunk works, and learned papers are written on how to encourage them.

Perhaps it's the only way some organizations can promote limited creativity, by consigning it to a twilight zone of semi-respectability. It shows how far many organizations must travel to really generate team creativity.

Short cuts – pinch the best

The impact of teams that do live by experimenting is far-reaching. Orson Welles, together with John Housemann and Joseph Cotten, created the radical Mercury Theatre company in New York. It's innovative style was a resounding success, and they produced a regular drama series on radio; that series broadcast the famous version of *War of the Worlds* that was so realistic it provoked national panic. The team was then snapped up by Hollywood and it's first film, *Citizen Kane*, has influenced film-makers ever since. People are wise to look to the experimenters for good product.

In fact most great business experiments owe their origin to some previous pioneer. There was absolutely nothing new about Green Shield Stamps, except how they were relaunched at the right moment. Richard Branson's Virgin Atlantic airline was a live experiment based on what he learned from Freddie Laker's experience. At the time many people thought Branson must either be mad to hire the failed Laker or was hiring him out of kindness.

At the start of a project act out a post-mortem. Imagine the worst. What are the implications?

In our fast team-building event a team creates a 3 or 4-minute video, bringing its 'nightmare scenario' to life. For several hours the team has enormous fun, devising, acting out and filming the worst possible situation.

Doomsday scenarios help a team to:

• Deal with its worst, unconscious fears.
• Accept that the chances of doomsday happening are remote.
• Reduce any false euphoria about a new activity.
• Emphasize that the team faces real choices.

Always end your hypothetical post-mortem by agreeing:

• Specific actions to prevent it really happening.
• A restatement of the ideal success scenario.

One of the Royal Shakespeare Company's greatest triumphs was its epic production of *Nicholas Nickleby*. It re-established the company's reputation on both sides of the Atlantic, with critics and public alike praising the experimental approach. However, the house style had actually been pioneered by the far smaller Shared Experience theatre company, whose own innovative approach in turn came from the storytelling techniques of traditional Eastern cultures.

What all this adds up to is that ACE teams live by experimentation. By giving people permission to keep saying 'Yes – now see how far you can take your idea', companies allow the team to build quickly and learn to be creative together.

" When you steal from one author, it's plagiarism; if you steal from many, it's research. "

Wilson Mizner

Permission to disagree constructively

Does this heading mean ACE teams should have lots of disagreements? We'd put it slightly differently. Along the way to creating something worthwhile, ACE teams tolerate wide differences of opinion, because creative solutions often emerge from combining two conflicting ideas. A team takes an idea or a theory, then tests it against an opposite or alternative version. Some companies even formalize this into a shoot-out, during which two opposing views present their case and the best one wins.

> " **For God's sake don't say 'Yes' until I finish talking.** "
> *Darryl F. Zanuck to an eager assistant*

Shoot-outs though are win/lose situations. Performing arts teams prefer a win/win situation, where from the resulting tension of disagreement comes the possibility of creating something new, incorporating both ideas.

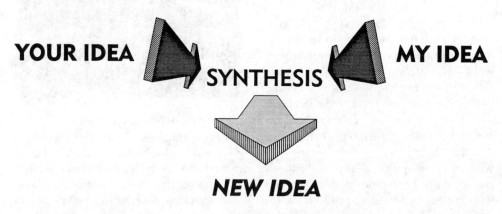

YOUR IDEA SYNTHESIS **MY IDEA**

NEW IDEA

Rehearsing any stage performance is a living version of this sort of constructive conflict. Faced by two actors with opposing ideas about a scene, the director's job isn't to make a cosy compromise that distils or weakens both ideas. A good theatre director will strive for synthesis – something completely new encompassing both positions.

In really effective business teams you earn your money by bringing to them a unique point of view. Otherwise it's like a set of clones working together – good for robotics, bad for creativity. Constructive disagreement doesn't undermine team alignment, it enhances it. Alignment, which stems from shared values, goals and vision, allows many conflicting ideas to emerge about how to get there.

The team leader can help devise situations in which this constructive disagreement can occur safely. Both Honda and BP have established systems to facilitate that kind of constructive disagreement. At Honda, there are meetings in which different teams publicly tackle a contentious issue. They have mastered the art of 'disagreeing without being disagreeable'. They know it's how the company keeps growing and maintains its quality.

When you start taking disagreement seriously as a creative force, there are lots of ways of encouraging it. IBM developed the idea of conferences held by people sitting and communicating by computer terminal. People could type in their comments without having to say who they were, and felt freer to disagree and put alternative views without seeming to be attacking anyone personally.

> " I like **Bartok** and **Stravinsky**. It's a discordant sound and there are discordant sounds inside a company. As president, you must orchestrate the discordant sounds into a kind of harmony. But you never want too much harmony. One must cultivate a taste for finding harmony within discord, or you will drift away from the forces that keep a company alive. "
>
> *Takeo Fujisawa, Honda's co-founder*

PLAY DEVIL'S ADVOCATE

Ask people in your team to take a point of view and present it from an alternative perspective – a customer, a competitor, a disgruntled supplier. Let the person be articulate, reasonable and persuasive.

The rest of the team does not defend the situation. Instead it tries to synthesize the two views into something different. You could do it 'in character' or 'role'. Act different people from other departments or companies.

'Hitchhiking' is where a team consistently builds on other people's ideas. When we have meetings in our own company, you will often hear somebody say: ' I've got a thought about this. Maybe it's a lousy idea, but I'll throw it in anyway, because I'm sure somebody will be able to take issue with me and build on it'. From the ensuing argument something creative invariably arises.

So let's sum up. ACE teams give permission for people to disagree constructively, which encourages people to be creative. It has to be disagreement in which people build on each other's ideas, and it's about learning to disagree without being disagreeable.

Permission to fail – 'It'll be all right on the night'

When a child is learning to walk, it inevitably falls over. Do we hurl abuse at it, tell it that next time it had better not fail or else? If we did, we'd have a population of adults crawling to work. No, we give the child permission to fail. We don't sanction terminal failure, which would happen if the child fell over and never got up again. We encourage the child to keep trying. We do so by focusing on a natural desire to walk anyway. The internal motive is so strong that the infant can take a lot of failures on the road to success. After bumps, tears and frustration, the child eventually gets there.

An ACE team is rather like an infant learning to walk, reaching for success through lots of falling and plenty of rehearsal. Organizations and team leaders, and the team itself, must learn to tolerate this kind of failure, which is not terminal.

What exactly is terminal failure? Let's look at the theatre again. A top team avoids being so 'way out' it could put the entire organization at risk. Running a large organization like the Royal National Theatre, for example, director Richard Eyre can experiment with a new team in any one of three different company theatres. Yet he knows exactly how much budget and energy to invest before collapse would threaten the entire operation. Whatever creative risks he takes, they must never jeopardize a theatre's life.

> **" If you don't instill in your people the ability to fail, they will never take risks. But when they fail there's no reason why they should take the whole ship down with them. "**
>
> *Michael Eisner – Head of Disney Corporation*

This constraint on Eyre is similar to what some companies call 'below the water line' decisions. As with a ship, you can make all kinds of mistakes, as long as you don't allow it to be seriously holed below the water line, when the chances of survival are small. Similarly, teams and managers need to be allowed a large range of freedom in the decisions they take. But no decision must be of the 'below the water line' variety, where it could sink the company.

So an ACE team is never reckless. It's willing to face failure in the interests of growth and change, but will rarely bet the company. That is, it will never willingly court a failure of such serious proportions as to damage either its own or the organization's chances of survival.

Marks & Spencer's move, for instance, to introduce franchising in certain countries was a major gamble. It moved the company well away from its traditional way of working, in which it retained tight control over its own retail outlet. Franchising was, however, a creative response to M & S entering certain markets, where its favourite way of working was not entirely effective. Embarking on franchising was risky yet never put the entire company at risk.

> **" Great orchestras rehearse. Great sports teams practise. To neglect practice and learning is, of course, foolish. But in today's business organizations we have little that fills the role of rehearsal or practice. We perform, perform, perform all the time and as a consequence, increase our ability to perform hardly at all. "**
>
> *Charlie Kiefer, researcher and consultant*

Hardly anyone likes or wants failure, least of all an ACE team. Yet only by willing to fail does it step into the unknown and develop its creative potential. If success had to be guaranteed, for example, no one would ever make a film – the odds are 10:1 on failure and worse for launching a successful shampoo.

One reason why theatre teams build quickly is that they keep so many balls in the air. Their skill is knowing how many they can keep up there without them all crashing to the ground. They do it by experimenting, and giving themselves permission to fail with some of them.

How do they know which ones they can allow to fail? They don't! They are like anyone else and are simply trying to discover how to succeed. Some of our most successful living talents have experienced disastrous flops: Spielberg's film *1948*, Woody Allen's *Star Dust Memories*, Alan Ayckbourn and Andrew Lloyd Webber's musical version of *Jeeves*, Peter O'Toole's *Macbeth*. Every great artist alive or dead has experienced an heroic failure.

> **" If you want to succeed double your failure rate. "**
>
> *J. R. Watson, IBM's founder*

The inevitable price of being a creative team is some failures along the way. You could argue that the more mistakes, the greater the chance of avoiding terminal failure and finding the route to success. Most companies, for instance, have to launch many products before they hit a real winner. It's how ACE teams handle the failure issue that makes them top performers.

There are some simple principles a team can adopt in learning to handle failure, one of which we've already met: **prevent failures from being terminal ones**. Another useful principle of handling failure is: **honour the effort**. This means doing what successful theatre teams do. Anyone attempting a new idea is given great encouragement, and tremendous support if they fail. It's a natural extension of the rehearsal process.

During the rehearsals, for instance, actors totally commit themselves to a particular interpretation, only to be told by the director or the other actors, 'It doesn't work, either at all or well enough'. The message to them is try something else! This nurturing leads to more, not less creativity.

In the training sessions we run in companies we sometimes ask teams to perform outrageously creative presentations. They do these under great pressure and to tough deadlines. When teams present, we ask everyone to applaud enthusiastically at the end of the performance, irrespective of the quality of the presentation. We're applauding courage and commitment – the content can always be changed at a later stage. Honouring the effort like this always stimulates people to do even better next time.

In the theatre mistakes can sometimes be extremely humiliating. The last response you want is people putting the knife in with 'I told you so' or 'You deserved it!' let alone further reprimands.

In too many businesses mistakes lead to direct or indirect punishment of those responsible, through firing, non-promotion and withdrawal of privileges. This is treating the failures as if they *are* terminal. This is why some 'product champions' who attempt to drive innovative schemes through a company often pay a personal price for failure – for them it does indeed become terminal.

For people wanting success, the humiliation of not winning is usually chastening enough. ACE teams and their leaders need to become good at honouring the effort. It builds a team climate, which gives permission to fail, without condoning it. You are not saying 'Well done for failing', you are saying 'Thanks for trying, now try again, and this time succeed!'

Here we come to our final rule of handling failure for ACE teams. ACE teams can afford

lots of mistakes **as long as they learn fast from them**. The economics of the performing arts forces an intolerance for continual failure. For example, the legendary film director Preston Sturges formed a team of comedy talent that produced a succession of hit shows. He was at the height of his fame as the first writer turned director when he made two films that flopped. The film industry regarded this not as a failure along the way, but as a terminal one and Sturges's career and team never recovered.

Similarly a repertory theatre director is rarely permitted more than two disastrous productions in a row. It takes a long time to build a loyal audience, which can be lost by a single turkey of a show. For its own good, the team knows it must learn, and learn quickly.

To sum up, ACE teams:

- Prevent failures from being terminal ones.
- Honour the effort.
- Learn the lessons fast.

For team leaders wanting a creative team, these principles hide an even simpler truth, that people are always bigger than their failures. That's why children walk.

When teams examine their failures, the tendency is to start blaming. Try a 'once removed' game:

- The team examines its mistake, but once removed – as if another team had made it and was paying for advice.
- As 'clients', the other team wants its information presented in a blame-free way, without picking on individuals as scapegoats.
- Tell them about:

How the team reacted to early warning signs.
The speed of team reaction.
How individuals were treated once the failure surfaced.
The measures taken to:

reduce the chance of any repetition,
eliminate the chance of any repetition.

Any good things to emerge from the experience.

ACT TWO - Scene 1 "START WITH YES!" - Permissive Encouragement

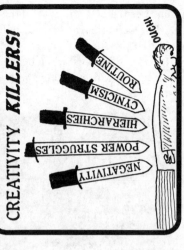

> **"In every job that must be done, there is an element of fun. Find the fun - and (click) the job's a game!"**
>
> *Mary Poppins*

Scene 2 - **'RIDING THE ROLLER COASTER'**
Creative Energy

Creative Energy

" **British music leads the way because we are always looking for something new and we are more prepared to take risks and break the rules.** "

Rob Dickens, chairman of Warner Music UK

Our two directors are talking on the phone . . .

MANAGING DIRECTOR:	*Oh dear, the truth is, things are really grim!*
THEATRE DIRECTOR:	*Sorry to hear that.*
MANAGING DIRECTOR:	*The team's deeply depressed. I can't really understand it.*
THEATRE DIRECTOR:	*What can't you understand?*
MANAGING DIRECTOR:	*How can they be so totally miserable, when only last week they were having more fun than I've ever seen any team having in my entire life.*
THEATRE DIRECTOR:	*Don't you think the two might be linked?*
MANAGING DIRECTOR:	*You mean – you can't have one without the other?*
THEATRE DIRECTOR:	*Exactly. ACE teams have lots of ups and downs. And they're often quite extreme. What's more, I think it's an essential part of the creative process. It's what happens when you try and excel, strive for star performance, reach for the impossible. It's often an intensive struggle.*
MANAGING DIRECTOR:	*Well, if it's this painful, I can see why most teams, most companies for that matter, don't bother trying. It's more comfortable settling for second best.*
THEATRE DIRECTOR:	*It may be more comfortable, but it's about as exciting as riding a flat roller-coaster! And ultimately there's very little satisfaction in striving for mediocrity.*

MANAGING DIRECTOR:	Like the joke about the English approach to the Olympics?
THEATRE DIRECTOR:	What d'you mean?
MANAGING DIRECTOR:	Go for bronze!
THEATRE DIRECTOR:	Yes. Well, I'm not one to advocate winning at all costs, but in my experience teams do best when they set impossible standards and dare to be different. And that has to mean releasing creative energy.
MANAGING DIRECTOR:	Which means, downs as well as ups!
THEATRE DIRECTOR:	'Fraid so.
MANAGING DIRECTOR:	Well, how do you handle it?
THEATRE DIRECTOR:	By understanding the process and allowing for lots of play and fun, and equally quite a bit of pain and struggle.

Going for gold

" **I'm a believer in the yin and yang of everything . . . a movie slate shouldn't be all safe bets. The business should not be about conviently giving the audience today what they wanted yesterday, but always making them reach just a little bit higher.** "

Brandon Tartikoff, recently appointed head of Paramount Studios

ACE teams always go through an intensive struggle to excel. But what's so special about this struggle? Don't all teams have to struggle?

The difference with ACE teams is they make exceptional efforts to go for gold. It's a creative drive to reach beyond mediocrity and mere competence. The team members don't necessarily work longer hours or dedicate their whole life to the team, although there may be intense periods when just about everything is subordinated to the team's hunger for star performance. When this creative energy is working, you see people and teams bristling with ideas and new ways of working. People feel closer together as a group, and there's also a greater willingness to rock the boat and challenge the cosy existence of other teams.

Creative energy sounds inspiring, doesn't it? When it's happening, you can see a team having periods of intense work charged with enthusiasm, balanced by periods of pain and struggle with perhaps even low morale.

Star performance is dramatic. When you watch massive upsurges of creativity, in which the group is highly productive and everything seems to go well, there's plenty of drama in it.

Play and fun

> **In every job that must be done, there is an element of fun. Find the fun – and (click) the job's a game.**
>
> *Mary Poppins*

Many teams play and have fun, but it's often confined to extra-mural activities, or they tend to channel it into activities such as conferences, team away-days or planning weeks. They're unwilling to allow it into the day-to-day activities of the work place. It's almost as if play and fun will contaminate the seriousness of the 'real work'.

There's seldom any effort to disguise these things in the performing arts. One of the crazier quirks of acting, for example, is that people work in terrible conditions for little pay. Why? While part of it may be a passion for expressing themselves, an important reason is they have enormous fun at it. There is tremendous childlike energy constantly around, with lots of playfulness.

Good teams are driven by a vision, and when they play and have fun with that vision, they're temporarily suspending their sense of reality. They enjoy themselves imagining a new triumph, toying with it, creatively designing it. Seeing this, some business people of course would say something like 'You're here to work, you're not paid to have fun and laze about having fantasies', which is why they can unconsciously prevent their teams from using their full creative energy.

Performers working in teams promote that sense of playfulness quickly, using plenty of ways which anyone in business can learn quite easily. A favourite technique that stimulates the sense of creative play amongst stage people is using IF.

> Having set realistic targets and a strategy for achieving them, try this creative exercise:
>
> • What would have to happen to meet double the target?
> • What would have to happen to meet ten times the target?
>
> It may be unrealistic, but in thinking about achieving the impossible, you may stretch your mind, challenge old assumptions, gain some useful insights and even tap into new reserves of team energy and enthusiasm.

Magic 'if'

We don't mean that tired old phrase 'If only . . .', which is something totally different. *That* kind of IF is an evasion. People say things like:

- If only we were more profitable, then we could afford better working conditions.
- If only our competitors were environmentally conscious, then we could be too.
- If only I had a better job, then I'd be able to show what I could do.
- If only I had a loving relationship, then I could express my feelings.

While there may be truth in all these, they really avoid action by blaming external events. They make a person or team solely reactive.

> **In everyday life 'if" is a fiction, in the theatre 'if' is an experiment. In everyday life 'if' is an evasion, in the theatre 'if' is the truth. When we are persuaded to believe in this truth, then the theatre and life are one. This is a high aim. It sounds like hard work. The play needs much work. But when we experience the work as play, then it is not work any more. A play is play.**
>
> *Peter Brook*

The kind of IF we mean is when you wonder what would happen if . . . all sorts of crazy things. Using IF in this way is playing with images. It's performed by a different part of our brain to the bit handling logic and reason.

Business has long used 'what if questions' to study different business scenarios, choose between alternative cash flows, review options. Spread sheets on computers now let managers play their own 'what if' games. Yet it's still mainly a specialist field, rather than a general resource for team creativity.

Teams can use IF to transform, to stretch the imagination to reach for something new and better. This method might seem unduly speculative and totally open-ended. You could ask millions of that sort of 'what if' question. Where does it start and end?

It starts where most games begin, with everyone being willing not to ask 'What's the use of it?' You just enjoy it for its own sake to see where it leads. That is, you start at random, which is incidentally where so many dreams begin.

But it's often also necessary to SEE what something would look like, HEAR what it would sound like and FEEL what sensations and experiences it arouses. You have to play with the image and then make it utterly real. That's what actors do every day in rehearsal. They create a character and build a scene by living out the future, acting out how it's going to be.

It is also the basis of our own fast team-building programme, The Producers. During two and half days the team members have fun playing with a common issue such as how to launch a new product, or creating a new company culture. They make videos of how they currently see and what they feel about the present situation, what would it be like if they

What if we each worked from home on at least one day a week? What if we each worked from

What if we were **10** times our present size, how would we be organised?

What if we made NO mistakes?

What if customers really came first?

What if we changed our end-of-year, how would that affect our accounting?

What if we functioned without a particular departments~

What if we changed the office around, how would we relate to each other?

What if we did it in $\frac{1}{2}$ the time?

did nothing – which is called the 'nightmare scenario' – and finally they play with designing what the ideal situation would look, feel and sound like.

Roger Hollis, Head of the Room Service Design Division of the Chessington-based Tricorn Group was asked by us to build an image of future success through describing his dream situation. He wrote:

'In five years time come looking for us! We'll be easy to find. The name will be the same but we will have moved a short distance. Located on the southern fringes of Central London we will be ideally positioned for close contact with most of our clients.

'You will know its us not by the exterior, shape or size of our offices but by the creative and dramatic input of our reception, imparting creative drive, informality and efficiency. Once seen never forgotten.

'Once inside you will get the impression of space. Some of the area is given over to showroom/roomsets and displays of past design work. The remaining area will be office space utilized but not fully occupied. A high proportion of staff will be out on site meeting with clients.

'The atmosphere will be characterized by 'hectic efficiency', resulting from a motivated and committed team most directly accountable to clients for the results of their activity. There will be very little resource allocated to bureaucratic and support functions. Wherever possible this is with sub-contractors.

'Motivation and commitment are also achieved not only through structural and managerial techniques but also less abstract factors such as worth-while profit share and share options; rewarding staff directly for their contribution in expanding the company. Naturally a company-wide share option scheme suggests that the company has recently been floated successfully on the USM [Unlisted Stock Market]. We achieved this level of growth by having a clearly defined strategy which the whole team understood and was committed to at the outset . . .'

The image Roger created formed the basis for developing a highly practical corporate strategy and later a business plan.

Build an image of what you would like your company, your team, your group to be in the future.
It is 5 years hence and you *have* already achieved what you set out to do. Get the rest of the team to question you as if it had already happened. (Perhaps you're being interviewed by a newspaper or magazine.)
You may not know all the answers but try describing the situation in as much detail as possible. It may produce some interesting and useful pointers.

(SUGGESTION)

Thus the team goes beyond IF and travels all the way to inventing a realistic picture of a great performance. Team members actually experience seeing, hearing and feeling success for themselves. For them it becomes stunningly real.

The whole process breaks through the barriers the left side of the brain puts up – the barriers of logic, reasoning and the denial of the reality of what is happening. Instead what the team is playing with becomes temporarily a reality and, using this, the team can start planning systematically how to make it happen.

There are many other ideas like this from the acting and performing world that can help business teams: for example IMAGING. You use images to help the team or person pinpoint where they are stuck. For instance, quite often people talk of making an organization 10 or 15 per cent more profitable or efficient.

But what about an image of the company ten times as big, ten times as efficient, or ten times as enjoyable to work in? Resistance to playing with the ideas shows the team is probably stuck, locked into a narrow image that prevents it reaching for the impossible.

When the limits are already firmly fixed in a team's collective thinking, it's hard to achieve something exceptional like star performance. This is where fun comes in. Fun gives permission for people's creative energy to begin flowing in new ways and unusual directions.

When Lyn Lavers was managing director of the business and computer magazine division of the EMAP publishing company, she ran a session during which the staff all dressed up in *Star Trek* uniforms. Their declared mission was to 'boldly go where no team has gone before'. It was highly productive and everyone also had an hilarious time.

" We don't stop playing because we grow old, We grow old because we stop playing. "

And there was the American computer firm that wanted to make learning about computers into a really exciting event. Its computer room had tall columns that carried the cables to the ceiling, and it was all rather depressing. So the company turned the whole place into a Hawaiian beach, made the columns into palm trees, and played Hawaiian music, and when people came in, they had flower garlands hung round their necks. People couldn't wait to learn!

There are so many ways teams can use their creative energy for fun and play. Some companies do it, but maybe only once a year. The staff of our local Lloyds Bank wear fancy dress every Christmas eve. It totally transforms the atmosphere of the bank. Customers actually smile and exchange a joke or a comment with the counter clerks.

Comic Relief events give people an excuse to do outrageous things because it's all in a good cause. And, in the US, consider the Sabre Institute, a charity dealing with people in great need. It works in many of the poorest of the third-world countries, trying to alleviate suffering. It is highly committed and faced with unsurmountable problems. It's a serious business. However, the Institute knows that if its staff didn't have fun doing their work, they would go mad. So if any of them get too serious at a board meeting, they are asked to put on a Groucho Marx nose, moustache and glasses. It may be a bit ridiculous, but the Institute is convinced it stops them getting pompous and morbid.

Michael Schuetzendorf, the General Manager of the London Hilton Hotel in Park Lane, identifies a turning point in the development of his organization. He took over the hotel and was concerned to strengthen the team spirit among the senior management. He asked us to lead a session to improve communications and team work. Towards the end he came in and said: 'I heard the sound of laughter. It was a marvellous sound. I knew then that we could turn it around. A team that can laugh together, can really go places'.

What all our examples show is how eager people are to experiment in using play and fun in order to put their creative energy to work. It's the child in us that is so useful for having fun. We had great natural playful instincts when we were young and learning to manipulate the world around us. We had the will to explore and were curious about everything. That part still exists, though often it lies buried deep within us.

Actors and performers also use humour to encourage play and fun to release the team's creative energy. It can provide a shift in perspective and make a team see its goals and problems in a new way.

> ## " Humour is one of the least understood and most valid tools of management and leadership. The appropriate use of humour can defuse, amuse, motivate, challenge and completely change the atmosphere. "
>
> ### Sir Brian Wolfson (Chairman of Wembley)

Humour allows us to give and receive feedback without being threatening. Sir John Harvey Jones provides a particularly British angle on this, arguing that much of what we say in Britain is indirect: 'We tend to be evasive. But sometimes you have to call a spade a bloody shovel – and the only way to do that without offence is to use humour'.

Humour also helps teams cope with the darker side of creative energy, when perhaps there isn't much around. The *Financial Times* once reported that the directors of the ITT company were collectively known as seagulls because, according to staff, 'They fly in, make a loud noise, eat your food, shit on everybody and fly out again'.

Often we find teams tapping their creative energy once they use their humour in some way. A group of insurance brokers we helped develop into a team summed up the creative experience as, 'thank goodness we regained our sense of humour'. The humour they shared helped the group become more cohesive, allowed them to work productively and helped them become more profitable as a commercial service.

Pain and struggle

Cyclists say 'There's no gain without pain', because you have to struggle to the top before the joy of flying downhill. Pain is also the darker side of creative energy.

> Take fun seriously! Ask the team 'when did we last have some fun together?' Ask them what is needed to create fun right this minute. *SUGGESTION*

Is pain unavoidable? By trying to avoid it, you negate the power of creative energy. What we're saying is that some struggle is necessary and shows that something new is occurring or about to do so.

So what is pain and struggle about? It concerns:

- The uncertainty of success.
- Being unproductive.
- Temporarily lacking insight or inspiration.
- Being lethargic and almost inactive.

We believe firms have to learn to handle these difficult periods in creative ways.

Take uncertainty, for instance. When a team tries to create something new, exceptional or different it embarks on an adventure, and not all adventures have happy endings. ACE teams know this but are still prepared to make the journey. Some firms, though, don't even want to start. For example, the Disney Corporation performed badly immediately after Walt's death because every new business opportunity was judged by the criterion of 'Will it do as well as Mickey Mouse?'

In addition, there's 'paralysis of analysis', where fear of uncertainty makes teams endlessly seek and dissect information as a substitute for action – when, say, they rely too much on market research rather than risking direct learning in the market place.

But sometimes we tend to dramatize the situation beyond its natural life, and wallow in the struggle. What fuels self-pity and wastes energy is thinking that suffering is all there is, that it's the end of the line. When teams reach that stage their response to uncertainty is usually a retreat into 'If only . . .'

Stage performers are very familiar with uncertainty. They know it's part of discovery and therefore accept it and the accompanying anxiety. On our presentation courses, even the experienced presenters admit how their nerves never go away as they face the uncertainty of performance. No matter how experienced they are, the anxiety and uncertainty remain.

Many performers, including Lord Olivier, Glenda Jackson and Ian Holm, have all described how the anxiety doesn't lessen as you become older and more experienced. It's a common experience for many professional performers to reach a stage in the rehearsal process where they think, 'I can't do this. It'll never work. I don't know how to act any more. My career is over'. Terrifying though these feelings are, as the years go on, you become familiar with them. They become a part of the creative process.

This is where a team is so useful. Having others around you to offer reassurance is invaluable. In this atmosphere admitting you're facing huge uncertainty can be turned into a strength not weakness. Honesty like that, needs to be respected and supported.

One of the dark sides of creative energy is that, following an intense period of activity, a team is bound to be less productive. Watching it apparently become sterile, doing nothing of note, can be enormously frustrating and baffling for onlookers. The natural temptation is to want to push the team even harder. And so many companies are intolerant of teams that have periods of low productivity. Perhaps they have found that pushing any team hard enough will always produce some results. The trouble is that this way promotes sustained star performance. Creative artists all suffer periods when nothing new or valuable happens. Sometimes these occasions are prolonged, but they are seldom as useless as they seem.

Sometimes it is just important to be able to talk about such frustrating and fearful periods, perhaps giving them a name:

' Tunnel of Despair'
' Dark Night of the Soul
' The Pits'
' Bermuda Triangle'

Don't try and change anything. Just let it be bad for a bit, and trust that something may come out of it.

This process can be hard to live with. Britain's most successful playwright, Alan Ayckbourn, is a clear example of this process of apparently unproductive periods. With a year to write a play, he often leaves it until shortly before rehearsals start, then writes it all in one go. The complete script is in his mind's eye.

In the early days when after a year of apparent inactivity he hadn't written a word, people panicked. Now people have learned to trust his process, for although he looks unproductive, something is happening all the time.

> " **The day I lose my stage fright is the day I give up.** "
>
> *Laurence Olivier*

Next time the team has to prepare a report, try building in a period for treading water. Instead of sending the report out immediately it's finished or constantly reading it for mistakes, let it lie fallow for a while.

Then come back and read it with fresh eyes. It is surprising how many mistakes jump out, or how additional and important points demand insertion.

When teams appear to be having unproductive periods, this is often when new lines of opportunity open up, new relationships are formed, new ideas and information gathered, and everything is being assimilated. It's like a plant waiting to burst forth just before the spring. It's important not to force it to sprout too soon. ACE teams learn to value these quieter, apparently unproductive aspects of their creative energy, just as much as the high spots .

For some teams, not performing well may cause gloom and despondency. Yet, without being obvious at the time, even the black moods serve a creative purpose:

- They stimulate some people to fight back and challenge the team mood, and so help to change it.
- They provide an essential and vivid contrast for future surges of creative energy – the periods of intensity when everything goes well.

Knowing the purpose of the bleak moods doesn't make them any more comfortable. Pain hurts! What keeps a team going is knowing that everything changes. Like talented actors, ACE teams learn to pace themselves, to be aware of where they are in the cycle of creative energy and to be active in handling it. ACE teams provide the environment in which creative energy in its positive and negative aspects can flourish.

When a team is in the downside of its creative energy cycle, who knows what it will take to make the breakthrough? While waiting for nature to take its course, teams can try and get nature moving, as shown in the adjacent suggestion box.

Creative energy is so essential to having a powerful team that it is surprising how little attention has been paid to it by organizations. This partly reflects a misunderstanding that confuses creative thinking with creative energy.

Creative thinking has been well explored by successful companies but remained confined to specialists and to seminars on how to generate new ideas. Creative energy, on the other hand, is a huge company resource, whose potential has seldom been fully exploited. The ways of tapping this potential are still evolving, which is why we have seen

Some tips for getting through 'Tunnels of Despair':

1 Take a break. Take five, take ten or preferably a day or two off. No good flogging a dead horse!
2 Do something different. Just stop! It's no good carrying on doing what you're doing at the moment. That's what got you stuck in the first place, so it's no good doing more of the same.
3 Draw or paint the situation as you see it now. You don't have to be great artists to express some of that despair visually.
4 Have a 'Dark Night of the Soul' session. All sit around and give yourselves a fixed time limit to say just how bad it is.
5 Share inspirations, as suggested in Scene 2.
6 Get a child in and explain why you feel so despondent. Really listen to his/her suggestions .

some serious attempts to translate how, say, sports teams develop and use their energy. Stage performers are certainly as good a resource, maybe a better one, for learning to handle creative powers, since this is what they do for a living.

When elderly, the painter Renoir suffered from arthritis. His great friend Henri Matisse watched sadly as Renoir, grasping a brush with only his fingertips, continued to paint, even though such movement caused stabbing pain. One day Matisse asked Renoir why he persisted in painting, enduring so much torture. Renoir replied: 'The pain passes, but the beauty remains'.

ACT TWO - Scene 2 "RIDING THE ROLLER COASTER" - Creative Energy

IMAGING THE FUTURE

RIDING THE ROLLER COASTER

of CREATIVE ENERGY

We all have our UP's ....

FUN AND PLAY

PAIN AND STRUGGLE

.... and *DOWN's*

CREATIVE ENERGY
means, not just thinking,
but.....

CREATIVE *ACTION!*

LEAVE SPACE...

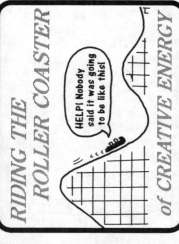

> **"Few people think more than two or three times a year. I have made an international reputation for myself by thinking once or twice a week."**
>
> *George Bernard Shaw*

Scene 3 - **'MORE THAN THE SUM OF THE PARTS'**
Using the Whole Person

Using the Whole Person

Our two directors are visiting the *Guinness Book of Records* exhibition . . .

THEATRE DIRECTOR:	*What are we doing here?*
MANAGING DIRECTOR:	*I remember you saying that visiting unusual venues was a good stimulus to creativity. What could be more stimulating than seeing the fastest, fattest, strongest and tallest humans, let alone the record for eating the most whelks while parachuting from a skyscraper, or something?*
THEATRE DIRECTOR:	*You certainly sound a bit more playful than last time we spoke.*
MANAGING DIRECTOR:	*Oh, yes, the team members are learning to take things in their stride. They're living life at such an intense level they don't think about it any more. In fact, I've just realized something . . .*
THEATRE DIRECTOR:	*What's that?*
MANAGING DIRECTOR:	*The complaints have changed.*
THEATRE DIRECTOR:	*What, you mean, they complain a lot?*
MANAGING DIRECTOR:	*No more than usual. People always complain, it's natural. I think most of them have it on their daily 'to-do' lists! No, I mean the content has changed. In the past it was things like 'I'm always stuck at my desk', 'Don't ask me, I'm just the financial manager', 'I don't feel my mind is stimulated much', or even 'People don't trust my hunches'.*
THEATRE DIRECTOR:	*They're all comments about not being personally fulfilled.*
MANAGING DIRECTOR:	*Yes, that's it precisely. A feeling that they have tremendous talent yet are using only a fraction of it.*
THEATRE DIRECTOR:	*A great waste.*
MANAGING DIRECTOR:	*It certainly was but it's changed. Now they are the sort of humorous complaints like 'I never knew this is what "creative accountancy" meant' or 'Hang on a minute, I'm a designer, what am I doing being*

	cost-conscious!'
THEATRE DIRECTOR:	*Sounds like they're really using more of themselves.*
MANAGING DIRECTOR:	*Oh yes. The truth is we're flying by the seats of our pants, using every bit of ourselves. I suppose we'll soon burn out, like you arty people. Live fast, die young – isn't that it?*
THEATRE DIRECTOR:	*Oh, you mean like Edith Evans, Ralph Richardson, Otto Klemperer, Sybil Thorndike, Ninette de Valois, Peggy Ashcroft, George Burns . . .*
MANAGING DIRECTOR:	*All right, all right. Point taken.*
THEATRE DIRECTOR:	*. . . And Sir John Gielgud won a BAFTA award for his performance in a really radical, way-out film by Peter Greenaway, in his eighties.*
MANAGING DIRECTOR:	*I suppose there are exceptions.*
THEATRE DIRECTOR:	*No, these are the norm. The exceptions are the few who burn themselves out. Medical and other research confirms that it's the active, fully involved people who stay the healthiest. The excitement of the creative process releases a feeling of being alive. Using people thoroughly means they blossom and often live longer.*
MANAGING DIRECTOR:	*So part of being a creative team is learning to use everyone as a whole person.*
THEATRE DIRECTOR:	*Right. That means using their minds, bodies, emotions, intuition, and even their sexuality.*
MANAGING DIRECTOR:	*Oh, I see. Talking of which, look at that exhibit there. Is that the biggest, fastest, shortest, longest or what. . . ?*

Orson Welles once gave a one-man show of Shakespearean readings in Phoenix, Arizona, and found only five people in the audience

'Allow me to introduce myself,' he said. 'I am an actor, a writer, a stage director of both films and plays, an architect, a painter, a brilliant cook, an expert on the Corrida, a conjuror, a collector, a connoisseur, an *enfant terrible* and an authority on modern art. How come there are so many of me and so few of you?' Then he walked off.

" It's my body. Thats what I work with. "

Gerard Depardieu

Use your body

In the theatre people use their bodies the whole time. It's an essential way of expressing themselves and linking thoughts to action. That may seem rather an alien idea if your job is to run a business team.

Yet some of the best business teams are in the construction, engineering and oil industries, where people are physically working together. Another example would be medical teams doing a surgical operation. They work with their bodies, and body contact is not so much a taboo as elsewhere. Sharing physical demands helps breed comradeship and bonhomie – which may sound like an argument for collective farms or forced labour when what we are really saying is:

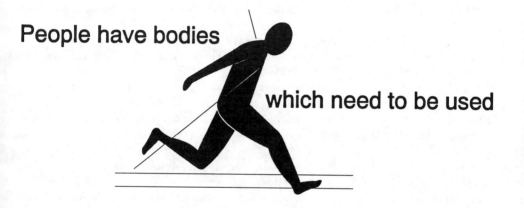

People have bodies — **which need to be used**

In E. M. Forster's short story 'The Machine Stops' the human race has evolved into blobs. They all live underground and only use their brains to operate a computerized control panel. That's not a million miles away from the business environment of many organizations!

Unfair? It's a fact that while we all need our bodies to go on living, many of us at work have no real outlet for physical expression. Meanwhile people mock those Japanese for insisting their employees start the day doing exercises or end with a session of Tai Chi.

Our main point is that people work better in sedentary jobs if they can also use their physical selves. Even geniuses need to do it. When Albert Einstein was tackling a difficult problem, he would rise and pace around the room. During this he invariably found the answer. It was as if the thinking process was insufficient. He had to create with his whole being.

Admittedly there are occasionally brilliant people who seem to defy this principle. The physicist Stephen Hawking remains highly creative, despite being confined to a wheelchair and almost immobile. In most cases, though, creativity and using our physical selves seem to go together.

This may be one reason to support Management by Walkabout (MBWA), the idea of continually moving around, away from the desk, to be in regular contact with people. Unfortunately management is more often MBSP – Management by Staying Put.

Teams work more effectively when they use their natural physicality. The solution may be playing sport together. It could be merely knowing that meetings often fail because people's creativity becomes table-bound. Standing up and moving around may break the deadlock. You could tear pages off a flip chart, spread them around the room, and ask people to mark up the pages and so on.

These simple actions can be shared by team members and may help break the inertia that so often slows teams down. Or a particular member of a team can regularly bring back new thoughts and ideas through using his/her physicality. Two members playing tennis, squash or golf together may find it can provoke new ways of thinking or looking at the world.

Rorey Caffyn Parsons, managing director of the successful Badshot Lea Garden Centre in Surrey, takes a regular long annual weekend to ski with another MD who runs a similar business. 'All day, going up those endless ski lifts, we do nothing but chat about garden centres!' Usually he returns with several good ideas to try out in his own business.

Some people compensate for a lack of physical expression during work by finding a personal way of using their bodies. John Reeve, the managing director of Sun Life Assurance company, every day climbs the ten flights of stairs to his office rather than use the lift.

Generally business is slow to recognize the need to promote the physical use of team members as part of team creativity. Many companies acknowledge the need indirectly by providing sports, dance or gym facilities, but these are 'add-ons' to the natural work process and, besides, many smaller companies cannot afford them. It is more important for the team to find ways of expressing themselves physically through and at work. When performing arts teams are stuck creatively, they may do a limber up and some vigorous exercises together. This seems to have relevance for all teams.

Another way is through presentations. Good ones use the physical abilities of a group, and companies are increasingly experiencing the benefits of this form of working. Teams are being asked to 'make a presentation' rather than merely submit a report. Presentations, for example, require people to stand up, which is enlivening for the audience and literally keeps the presenters on their toes. There are many creative ways for making the presenting task more physical.

When presenting the findings of our own survey on management potential, we needed to give the invited audience many facts and figures. Rather than slides or overheads, we used physically expressive ways of communicating the information. For example, people

from the audience were asked to represent percentages, becoming 'human bar-charts'. We also used coins and other objects in the room to show results about motivation or potential. Not only did everyone have fun, they also absorbed the information more easily.

While it's important to use ourselves physically, there's always a danger that we overdo it. Stress results from using our physicality wrongly. Muscles tense for prolonged periods, which also triggers behaviour that can undermine a team, such as aggression, impatience, lethargy or withdrawal.

An important task for a team is handling stress, e.g. by insisting its members take regular breaks and even use their holidays fully. The many meditative techniques from yoga to martial arts are all designed to harness and focus individual and group physical energy. The more successful the team, the greater the need to counter an excess of 'doing' at the expense of 'being', which ultimately kills creativity.

> " Life is not having and a getting; but a being and becoming. "
>
> *Mathew Arnold*

Use your mind

Dancers or opera singers seem mainly concerned with the physical act of expression through their bodies. Yet most good performers also want what detective Hercule Poirot would call something to stimulate 'ze little grey cells'.

If business teams are also going to be creative, they too need to use their intellectual resources to the full. While there should be a bias for action, we need to watch for situations in which

> " When I talk to him, I fell like a plant that's been watered. "
>
> *Marlene Dietrich on Orson Welles*

people's minds are so focused on doing and implementation that they become unresponsive to anything else.

DISSENTING VOICES

" **Supreme common sense is worth a great deal more than intellect. Effective managers have a great deal of common sense allied with a lot of drive.** "

Sir Michael Edwardes

" **The biggest single handicap a person can have is to go to university.** "

Sir James Goldsmith

> Often in teams people get stuck voicing the same ideas over and over.
> Try using humour to cut through the deadlock. Talk of 'broken records' or 'TV repeats' as a friendly way of telling people to move on.

Thinking requires space, room to breathe, time to be – just what is denied to many teams. Equally there's always a danger of being over-intellectual at the cost of common sense. Is the team going beyond using people's intellect and becoming merely intellectual? Spot the signs on the next page.

Stage performers have many stories of hours spent in rehearsals 'just talking' – but the talk has been over-intellectual, removed from the real experience of creative action, and therefore stultifying. Being over-intellectual is a great way to avoid any creative action. It's essential to watch for those times when the team spends hours nitpicking or wrapped in mindless detail. ACE teams find ways to use people's intellect, not leave it to rot.

" **Few people think more than two or three times a year. I have made an international reputation for myself by thinking once or twice a week.** "

George Bernard Shaw

An important way is through a team culture that is always looking for and at new ideas. That may seem wishful thinking – either a team is open to new ideas or it's not – yet all teams can become more open to new ideas if they stimulate people intellectually and raise new creative possibilities.

People are always *reasonable*

Excessive jargon or clichés

Everything de-personalised little use of "I"

Lengthy academic or abstract discussion

Self righteous or justifying

Wordy statements

Is your team over-intellectual?

> " **The mind is like a parachute – it works best when it's open.** "

There are many books and training courses to assist teams and their members to think creatively. Path-breakers such as Edward de Bono and Tony Buzan have contributed much to our understanding and ability to use our intellect creatively.

Some successful ways to loosen the intellect and push team creativity include:

- **Mind-mapping** - a way of linking ideas, facts and information in the same way that the brain works, non-sequentially. Mind-maps have been written about extensively, and are regularly used by teams.
- **Random associations** - a way of letting our subconscious take over by deliberately exploring connections between non-linked ideas.
- **Use of symbols** - a way of encapsulating situations, processes, problems and so on, using symbols and then exploring how these give fresh insight or creative inspiration .
- **Brainstorming** - a systematic way of collecting up a mass of new ideas and then sorting them into some useful order so they can be evaluated and selected for further development.
- **Different hats** - a way of getting people to see situations, problems or challenges from a different perspective: people play different roles, dependent on what hat they are wearing.

Much creativity comes from making unusual or even bizarre connections. Here's an unusual one that might be fun at an appropriate moment:

Ask each team member to set a work problem for the others. It should be communicated in a creative way, such as a crossword puzzle or a riddle; or perhaps as a reference to historical events or classical or modern literature. For example, 'What can Darwin's theory of evolution tell us about our marketing plan?', 'How could we relate our production system to the success of the Roman Legions?' or 'What does Orwell's *Animal Farm* tell us about our organizational structure?'

It sounds off the wall, far removed from that perennial 'bottom line', which is precisely why it works.

To extend ourselves beyond the rigid and sometimes tyrannical processes of our left brains – the logical, rational part of ourselves – we also need to stimulate the right brain with feelings, sensations, movement, pictures and fresh air.

We live in mental boxes of our own and others' creations. Break out of the box and there's a sense of freedom. However, the job of the left side of the brain is to make another box, so the drive to think originally is a never-ending process of breaking boxes. The great thing about working in a team is that each member can accept responsibility for giving the others a good kick up their assumptions!

" You can't teach an old dogma new tricks. "

Dorothy Parker

Use your emotions

Creative teams also engage people's emotions. The psychologist Abraham Maslow looked into why certain people seemed to fulfil themselves more than others. He decided that creativeness was at the heart of it, and such people were less afraid of what other people would say or demand or laugh at. They could let themselves 'be flooded by emotion'.

Emotion is another fairly alien concept to many business teams. Many prefer to push emotions into the background, which may be why they are not star performers. As we hinted in our earlier section on relationships, you can't run a team or a company without using and tapping people's feelings.

Some of the most successful team leaders know how to excite and engage people's emotions to the full. There's an obvious connection here with the leader's ability to inspire people. Management thinker Peter Drucker once observed that companies ought to be run like the Girl Guide movement. In the Guides people devote enormous personal energy and time to the cause, love every moment and do it for nothing!

Teams that can tap into people's emotions are very powerful. Take Sarah, who works for the go-ahead Oddbins wine group. She told us how she got such a buzz from working in the company's stores and selling to customers that long after she had been promoted and moved to headquarters she continued working in a store at weekends without pay.

Just how did Oddbins make that happen? Mainly through producing a climate where people felt able to express themselves, share strong feelings and, as Sarah herself said, 'Make us feel we're one big family'. And that's in a company with a multi-million pound turnover and hundreds of employees.

So ACE teams make room for feelings to be expressed, because that makes the team more creative, alive and healthier. The connection between health and expressing emotions is now widely accepted. Certainly those who supress anger or who dwell on anxieties are more likely to develop ulcers, hernias and back pain.

We are not advocating daily temper tantrums! We do think teams need to establish their own way of blowing off steam. Members must know they can share their emotions about an issue without having them surppressed. In too many work environments this is taboo, particularly in open plan offices.

Open plan offices seem to stifle emotional expression through promoting a hushed atmosphere where strong, loud or sustained disagreement becomes anti-social. Teams using them become so practised at dodging conflict that when they cannot, the reverberations can seem like the end of the world.

The performing arts have long known that using and responding to feelings is a powerful creative force in a team. Musicians and dancers say how they can sense a composer's mood. Actors tap into their own deepest feelings to interpret a character's emotional

Try using the 'safety valve' idea mentioned in Act One Scene 3 (p. 66) and having it as the first item on the team's regular agenda – with a 5-minute time limit. *(SUGGESTION)*

People are asked to express how they are feeling and what might get in the way of them being effective right now.

This can seem strange and artificial at first, but the whole team soon gets used to it and sees the benefits. It requires really listening and responding to what people say. To have some fun you could:

- Ask everyone to draw a symbol for how they feel.
- Distribute a page showing scores of different faces all expressing different emotions and ask people to point to the one closest to how they are feeling right now.
- Go round the group at the beginning and end of a meeting and ask each person to offer one word that sums up how they are feeling.

emotional journey in a play, and affect other actors in the process.

> **" Seeing's believing, but feeling' the truth. "**
>
> *Thomas Fuller (1732)*

In business too, awareness of what may be happening inside other people is equally effective in helping the team draw the best from everyone. But the process is not usually sufficiently high on the agenda.

> **" You have to get to the stage where managers don't want to stop for lunch. You want people to leap up and down and feel things. You want them to get emotionally involved because if they're not, you're not even discussing the right subject. "**
>
> *Sir John Harvey Jones*

Use your intuition

> **" I can still remember the very spot on the road, whilst in my carriage, when to my joy, the solution occurred to me. "**
>
> *Charles Darwin*

Much of what a team does is done on intuition, although people wrap it in more acceptable names, such as common sense or experience. How do you encourage a team to use the members' intuition? One way is by making intuition respectable, for example through helping the team recognize that the most innovative experiences consist of strong intuitive elements that are believed to stem from the right side of the brain.

In business there's still distrust about helping people to be more intuitive. It's a messy area nobody really understands, compounded by uncertainty, ambiguity and sometimes the totally inexplicable. No wonder people are suspicious.

Science can't explain exactly what happens when we have a sudden insight. Despite research on the electro-chemical processes of the brain, our knowledge about intuition is primitive. Yet common experience, particularly from the performing arts, suggests that creative action requires our intuitive abilities.

In our work with companies we are tempted sometimes to suggest that if teams want more use of intuition, they should rely more on women. The latter often seem far more comfortable than men with intuition, using it creatively and taking risks with it. However, many men are highly intuitive too. Probably all teams would simply benefit from having a good mix of both men and women, and not be almost wholly composed of men, as are so many business teams.

> While lying in bed before going to sleep, think about a specific problem.
> In your imagination create for yourself a problem-solving room. Make it fantastical.
> The room can be of any shape, size and situation. It has magical resources, such as video screens that can show any event from history, and machines that will show you the future, and a telephone on which you can phone any person living or dead and talk to them.
> PLAY with the problem in this room. Enjoy letting crazy things happen. Then go to sleep. When you awake, see if any insights arise.

Another way of encouraging teams to use their members' natural intuition is by showing the team how intuition can best be mobilized. In other words, by giving them practical experiences of putting intuition to work, for example by taking a problem and suggesting that at some level they already have the answer, and the job of intuition is to find it. It's rather as if someone has misplaced an item in a filing cabinet and by continuing to search they eventually locate it. Instead of asking 'What is the answer?', or 'Will we ever solve this?', the team just assumes the intuitive part of themselves already knows and can unlock the door to important solutions.

What may be keeping the door shut is resistance from the subconscious, with its babble of memories, thoughts and emotions. Until these are quieted, intuition may not be able to work. This is why teams can make so much better use of their intuition when, despite organizational pressure for action, results, instant decisions and being seen to be busy, they find time and space to nurture inner calmness. We've touched on some ways to do this already, such as encouraging new ideas, using imagery, analogy, dreams, drawing, poetry and meditation.

When developing a role in rehearsal, many actors will talk about 'having a **feel** for the character'. Their job is to create a recognizable and real human being from descriptions and dialogue written on a page. It's a challenging, creative task. Actors gain a sense of what the character might be like and then try the persona out in rehearsal. The 'sense' comes from a period of mulling the problem over – night and day. Then an image or idea that could be the basis for a fully developed characterization might occur. For Anthony Sher's award-winning portrayal of Richard III, it was the image of a bottled spider. Beryl Reed talks about getting a feel for the character's feet: 'Get the feet right and the rest will follow!' She works at an intuitive level of understanding about people.

Musicians have a similar intuitive feel for a piece of music, often believing they are in direct communication with the composer, even though he may be long dead. By allowing the music to touch them and by spending a lot of time in contemplation, they experience intuitive flashes. Anybody who is open to them can receive them.

Meditation is still regarded by many business people as a freaky activity with little relevance to profit-making organizations. A more prosaic description would be focused concentration or mind-clearing. It could be as simple as having a vision, a guided fantasy, or following certain sorts of music.

ACE teams do not have closed minds and are willing to try anything which helps them achieve star performance.

> **"Reason's last step is the recognition that there are an infinite number of things which are beyond it."**
>
> *Pascal*

Next time the team is stuck on a problem, and you want to try something different, play a piece of your favourite soothing music.

Ask everyone to sit still, forget the problem, and also ignore any other thoughts that enter their heads.

Explain the music will last only 5 minutes, and no one should talk during that time.

Suggest that every time a thought pushes its way forward demanding attention, they should acknowledge its presence but then send it on its way – like a passing cloud – and return to focusing on the music.

If people want to close their eyes and get more comfortable, say that this is all right with you.

Play the music quietly, stopping it after 5 minutes, allow people time to 'come back' into the present, then ask if anyone wants to talk about the problem once more. Almost certainly the thinking of the team on the particular issue will now be different, more creative and probably productive.

Absurd? Not businesslike? Unacceptable in the work place? Perhaps, but it takes only 5 minutes, and meanwhile the team could have wasted three times that much time on struggling with the issue.

Sexuality

Watch great stage performers, of any age, and you are hit immediately by their sexuality. Sexual energy is a tremendous source of power, and, as you'd expect, is inseparable from creativity.

Sexuality is another taboo area in most organizations, one that is rarely discussed openly. Yet it's one of the major driving forces behind how people relate to each other. Of course it's also taboo at work because sexual harassment is rife and sexual discrimination is prevalent. Often the only way people can express this energy is through smuttiness.

In their zeal to reduce sexual harassment some employers have made it virtually a crime to acknowledge people's sexuality and differences. Their teams are potentially less dynamic as a result, and team members less fully functioning as people.

We're generally more comfortable with sexuality being up there on the stage than in there at the team meeting. Since sexuality is part of every one of us, you cannot really confine it to before 9 am and after 5 pm, or whatever hours the business expects one to work.

Teams can learn to use sexuality even in the work place. It's significant that the word POTENTIAL, which so many organizations are striving to release, comes from the root word POTENCY. Its formal definition is 'Power, strength, vigour. Power to intoxicate. Sexual efficacy'. Thus if we want to release people's potential, we must find ways to use all their powers, including their sexuality.

In the 1980s 'sexy' became a vogue word. Many sectors of the business world could talk of nothing else. There were sexy cars, sexy ideas, sexy shares, sexy deals, sexy projects, sexy profits. It was a clumsy way of trying to express an excitement about certain areas of work. People were truly 'turned-on' by various aspects of their jobs. It was an attempt to liberate libidinous energy. We repress our sexual energy at our peril. If people could only talk about it openly, without all the frightening implications, it might be possible to harness that energy.

"They can't censor the gleam in my eye."

Charles Laughton

When someone is giving a presentation, for example, it's one of the first unconscious assessments that the audience makes. Before people even open their mouths to deliver the latest sales figures, or next year's budgetary targets, the audience is unconsciously reacting sexually. Presenters often feel more effective and powerful if they feel good about their own personal attractiveness. They release a compelling energy. So for a team to use its sexual energy an essential requirement is **acknowledge gender differences**.

For example, one way that sexual differences are suppressed in business teams is a refusal to acknowledge the existence of the other person as a sexual being. In some teams if a woman member of the team looks particularly smart one day, no male team member says anything complimentary. Or if a man wears a particularly daring tie or a smart new suit, the women in the group studiously refrain from complimenting him.

Sexual differences can also heavily influence a team approach to issues. Women and men may sometimes see situations from a very different perspective. One of the authors once managed a team of six senior managers, all of whom were women. They often commented on how, as team leader, the author was giving a highly masculine interpretation of a situation or problem. What was valuable was the willingness of the team to talk about gender differences and use these creatively.

> How can a team acknowledge gender differences and use these creatively? Try exploring issues such as:
>
> • What are the gains from having/not having a woman (or women) on the team?
> • What are the gains from having/not having a man (or men) on the team?
> • Which members of the team seem to use their natural sexuality, e.g. male dominance, aggression, charm, passivity, to get their way?
> • How does it feel to be a woman (or man) on the team and always outnumbered by men (or women)?
>
> Note: It may be helpful to use the help of an experienced team facilitator to undertake this suggestion.

ACE teams find their own formula for acknowledging sexual differences and sexual energy to enhance the team's well-being.

We've talked about using all of a person within a team, their physicality, intellect, emotions, intuition and sexuality. Yet these are not easily divisible into handy compartments. We're really referring to obtaining a balance. Increasingly doctors are returning to a more holistic approach, rather than being just body mechanics dealing only with a single symptom. Similarly, with individuals, teams and whole organizations, all the ingredients of using the whole person need to be integrated into performance for it to be fully creative.

" I want to be thoroughly used up when I die; for the harder I work the more I live. I rejoice in life for its own sake; life is no brief candle to me. it is a sort of splendid torch that I've got to hold up for the moment. I want to make it burn as brightly as possible before handing it on to future generations. **"**

George Bernard Shaw

It's not by chance that we talk about the 'whole' person. Teams function best when the people in them feel 'whole'. That means that their lives are in balance. They have relationships that fulfil and nurture them, a sense of self-esteem, time off for recreation and a sense of proportion. As individuals they are more than the sum of their parts – as members of an ACE team, their talents multiply!

ACT TWO - Scene 3 "MORE THAN THE SUM OF THE PARTS" - Using the Whole Person

...use your MIND

as well as your MATTER....

Makes a WHOLE lot of difference to a TEAM.

A WHOLE PERSON

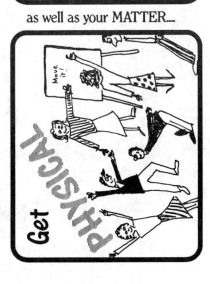

Get PHYSICAL

Move it!

Use your INTUITION

I follow my hunches.

As I thought....

...Sexual Energy makes POTENTIAL - POTENT.

$$1 + 1 + 1 +$$
$$1 + 1 + 1 +$$
$$1 + 1 + 1 +$$
$$1$$
$$= 10$$

Go forth and multiply......

An ACE team has PASSIONS....

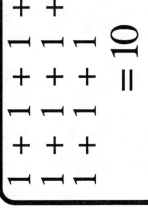

...even if it means OPEN HEARTED SURGERY!

Act Three: **EXPLORING**

Act Three: **EXPLORING**

PROLOGUE

PROLOGUE

> **"Do not follow where the path may lead. Go instead where there is no path and leave a trail. "**

It is not enough for an orchestra to play splendidly in rehearsal, or actors to produce a stunning performance at the dress rehearsal. The next level of growth, achievement and success is always with their audience.

It's always the audience that counts. All the alignment and creativity don't add up to a string of beans unless the audience approves. When a cast finally meets its audience, it's the final test. It's no different in business, though we may call the audience by different names, such as customer, consumer or client.

A team facing its audience is entering a new realm. This happens when ACE teams have got their internal processes working well and productively. Alignment and creativity are a way of life and yet there's more. The team now looks outside itself to explore how to make yet further impact in its chosen arena.

Every encounter with an audience is stepping into the unknown. It's why live theatre is so exciting. Anything can happen. What was safely planned in rehearsal is now tested in front of an audience. You may have rehearsed a play for 4 weeks, with a cast of ten people, got it to the point where you are totally satisfied and then another cast of, say 800 people, join you for the event.

This is exploration. As Columbus, Marco Polo and many others knew, travelling into the unknown produces surprises. You may discover a paradise or you may land in deep trouble. So it is for performers. So it is for ACE teams of all kinds. It's a risky business. There is always the possibility of failure. However, trail-blazers also create the potential breakthrough that sets them apart from others.

> **"Life is either a daring adventure, or it's nothing. "**
>
> *Helen Keller*

When Argos Catalogue shops opened some years back, for example, they were derided for breaking with British retailing tradition. Several hundred stores later, plus healthy profit margins, a new tradition of selling had been born. ACE teams that have reached the exploring stage of their development go beyond what the present rules say will work, and start making their own.

In 1973 when the world was hit by an oil shortage and sudden rise in prices, the 'rules' seemed to imply that growth for oil companies was over. Most oil companies were caught with their pants down – except the Royal Dutch Shell organization.

The Shell team had realized that improbable events could occur without warning and would demand not merely being aligned and creative in response, but also being willing to explore the unknown. It had prepared several different future scenarios from boom or bust to constrained growth. When the latter in fact followed, the Shell team was positioned to exploit the shortage. The company grew from number eight to number two during the 1970s.

> ## "The trouble with Cecil is that he always bites off more than he can chew – and then he chews it."
>
> *William de Mille, on his brother Cecil*

ACE Teams need to test themselves in the world, using their alignment and creativity as guides. An exploring team will pursue the following:

SCENE 1   'START WITH AN EARTHQUAKE' – Spirit of adventure
SCENE 2   'WHO DUNNIT?' – Growth and discovery
SCENE 3   'APPLAUSE, APPLAUSE' – Wholehearted appreciation

> **"Don't be afraid to take a big step if one is indicated. You can't cross a chasm in two small jumps."**
>
> *David Lloyd George*

Scene 1 - **'START WITH AN EARTHQUAKE'**

Spirit of Adventure

Spirit of Adventure

"What we want is a story that starts with an earthquake and works its way up to a climax."

Sam Goldwyn

Sounds of rotor blades, swirling wind and our two directors are seen strapped inside a helicopter, which, with a roar, takes off.

THEATRE DIRECTOR:	*I've never flown in one of these before. I'm not sure I like it.*
MANAGING DIRECTOR:	*Come on – you've been talking about being adventurous and stepping into the unknown.*
THEATRE DIRECTOR:	*Sure, but we've all got our scare thresholds!*
MANAGING DIRECTOR:	*You'll get used to it. Besides, I haven't just brought you on a joy ride.*
THEATRE DIRECTOR:	*Not sure 'joy' is the word I'd use.*
MANAGING DIRECTOR:	*You're here for some exploration. We've got a big event today, when the team are launching a new project. They're facing the customers for the first time. It's a crucial meeting. They'll have to perform at their very best, to really make an impact.*
THEATRE DIRECTOR:	*It sounds like a 'first night' – I know what that feels like. Think you're ready?*
MANAGING DIRECTOR:	*Hope so, we're well rehearsed – got a great spirit. But we're going to have to support each other 100 per cent.*
THEATRE DIRECTOR:	*And really focus on the customers. In fact you've got to turn all your team-building work inside out.*
MANAGING DIRECTOR:	*How do you mean, 'inside out'?*
THEATRE DIRECTOR:	*Well, you've got to take all that you've developed – vision, values, the way you relate to each other and your creativity – and direct it outwards instead of inwards. To make a difference, you need to start transferring your attention off yourselves and on to your audience or, in your case, customers .*

MANAGING DIRECTOR:	*Absolutely.*
THEATRE DIRECTOR:	*Then you'll know whether all the hard work and preparation has been a roaring success or an absolute disaster.*
MANAGING DIRECTOR:	*Precisely . . . exciting isn't it?*
THEATRE DIRECTOR:	*Terrific, I can see Tower Bridge and the docks.*
MANAGING DIRECTOR:	*No, I meant what's happening with my team!*
THEATRE DIRECTOR:	*Sorry! Yes, now you've got to go beyond your own boundaries and show a real spirit of adventure.*
MANAGING DIRECTOR:	*Flying high.*
THEATRE DIRECTOR:	*Yes . . . we are, aren't we.*
MANAGING DIRECTOR:	*I meant the team, being adventurous, flying high, going to the edge and all that.*
THEATRE DIRECTOR:	*Oh right! I suppose it must be different for every team.*
MANAGING DIRECTOR:	*Meaning?*
THEATRE DIRECTOR:	*Well, the basic elements arc the same: Trying to make an impact, delivering peak performance and taking risks. Yet each team has to explore them in its own unique way.*
MANAGING DIRECTOR:	*Sounds a challenge.*

"When you reach the top, that's when the climb begins."

Michael Caine

Make an impact

A team that is aligned and creative is ready to use its spirit of adventure and put it to practical use – beyond its own organizational boundaries.

With clear purpose and a sense of direction it can make an impact in its chosen area. Whether it's a sales or a production team, a systems or an executive team, it attempts to make a significant change somewhere. There are many ways a team can do this. Some achieve it with great style and razzmatazz, others may be *quietly* exceptional.

There are no prescribed rules to follow. ACE teams always break the mould and find their own particular style. If you like, it's exploring how to apply creativity in the outside world. It is nebulous because a team going for impact is like a successful stage company determined to capture an audience's attention and get results. There's a willingness to make a difference, though each team does so in a unique way. It's adventurous, because, to be exceptional, you must be prepared to go beyond 'just good enough'. So making an impact can mean building outside relationships, communicating values beyond the team to its market place, developing a high profile with those it is affecting, and showing off its superlative service. Let's look at these one by one.

Relationships

Everything we said earlier about relationships in Act One Scene 3 now applies externally. What's the point of trying to make an impact through building relationships within the team if you aren't going to make an impact through building relationships beyond it?

Make a list of the internal and external customers with whom the team has most contact. Evaluate how good your relationships with them are. How would you characterize the relationships, e.g. friendly, businesslike, homely, confronting, fun, difficult, helpful, boring?

Try using metaphors or similes to throw more light on the relationships: e.g. our relationship is like . . .

• The USA and the Soviet Union during the Cold War.
• Two athletic teams in the same Olympic squad.

What would you wish the relationships to be?

Building outside relationships has always been a key principle within our own company. Our clients and team of associates have always commented on the quality of those relationships. We deliberately take that spirit out into the world with us. We do relatively little advertising, the bulk of our business being generated through the relationships we build with clients.

There's nothing cynical about this. We don't form relationships to milk business from customers. We genuinely enjoy people. It's a pleasure for us to spend time with our clients. The feedback we receive is that they enjoy the relationships too. We have always held the belief that in the long-term it benefits both parties - and it is proving to be so.

Sometimes completely new training and development programmes are created from social conversations with our clients – rather than our producing a product and then having to 'sell' it to the market. Our external relationships help promote new products.

One feature that helps create such external relationships is having clarified and made a commitment to certain team values.

Communicating values beyond the team

Values are not only useful within the team, as discussed earlier, they can also make an impact on the market place. We once sent a team to meet a major pharmaceutical company, created by a merger 3 years earlier. The team began by producing the potential client's own company report, which contained some clear corporate values. The potential client explained it was still early days and these values were still not fully working. Next the team produced our own company brochure to show how similar our core values were, and made the point that, even though we were 'small fry', we were at least aligned on values and could contribute to reinforcing theirs. We got the contract!

On a far bigger scale, when BP set up its 'Culture Change' programme in 1990, it went to great lengths to communicate the core values to the staff. When the message came down from the board to 'spread the word', back came the question 'Who to?' What people wanted to know was, 'Do we tell our competitors about our commitment to certain values? Won't it lose us our competitive edge?'

The question showed a misunderstanding about the place of values in an organization or a team. Values are things you are extremely proud of. Using them gives you added impact both with internal staff and the external world. Exploring how your values relate to people and organizations outside your own boundaries is extremely challenging. You certainly need a spirit of adventure to do it.

It gives the team a much broader horizon and explains why the phrase 'stakeholder' has entered the language. Stakeholders are all the people who relate to the company. In BP's case it was its employees, suppliers, customers, the community and its shareholders. Everyone was seen as needing to hear about the company's new statement of values. After all, BP's principles and values underpinned its vision. To achieve the vision, values had to be communicated.

So to sum up, a team makes an impact through building external relationships, and that includes sharing and communicating its values. In doing that it begins to go beyond the company boundary towards a high profile.

Developing a high profile

The few in the performing arts who become stars do so because they bring a distinct sense of self to their work. Their personalities shine through. Whether you like them or not, it's hard to forget them. Star teams also need a strong group personality, even when individual members may have a low profile. This helps others, inside and outside the organization, to relate to them.

A team with a clear and distinct identity is visible and seen to be accountable for its work. Yet aren't there teams that operate in the background and are sometimes near invisible? Perhaps, but invisible to whom? Certainly not to those affected by their work. Star performers are willing to be known, and for them there is no hiding place.

As with making an impact, ACE teams are hungry to have a high profile where it counts, with their customers or those they serve.

> **"Teamwork is consciously espoused but unwittingly shunned by most people in business because they are deathly afraid of it. They think it will make them invisible."**
>
> *Srully Blotnick, in The Corporate Steeple Chase*

Spend some time looking at what's special about the team. How would a journalist characterize your team? Dynamic? New? Steady? Brave? Innovative? Sharp?

Perhaps you could give your team a name. When the culture shift happened in the American Insurance company Paul Revere, teams gave themselves names. The actuarial team called themselves 'The Class Act'. What could you be?

SUGGESTION

Showing off superlative service

Being adventurous also means seizing every opportunity to make an impact. Service is a perfect way of doing that, and people never forget when it is outstanding.

The staff in one hotel run by the Marriot Corporation seized an opportunity to show superb service when a guest rang room service and asked for refreshments. When there seemed problems in getting what she wanted, she rang off in annoyance. A few moments later a hotel supervisor knocked on the door. 'Excuse me', she said. 'I understand you may not be happy with our service, is there anything I can do to help you.'

The hotel guest began to cry. Her mother was ill in another part of the country and she had just spent an hour trying to book a place on the last plane leaving that day, to get home. There were no places available and the last plane was leaving shortly. She had given up in frustration and that's when she had rung room service.

The hotel supervisor listened and acted. She used the hotel's commercial muscle to persuade the airline to find a place on the plane for the guest. Not only that, she even arranged to have it delayed briefly so the guest could get to the airport. She helped pack the guest's bags, gave her some packed food for the journey and arranged transport to the airport. At the other end she organized transport so that the guest was whisked to see her mother in hospital. She arrived in time, and the mother died the next day.

You cannot simply buy that kind of adventurous spirit. What if the senior hotel management had condemned the expenditure as excessive? It came from building a team prepared to make an impact, willing to show its vision of superlative customer care in action. The team's impact more than paid off; the story has become a legend in the hotel trade and has more than repaid Marriot's outlay from the original decisions.

Using service to make an impact is a bit like showing off. Adventurous teams are willing to do that and even relish it. They are willing to be centre stage with light blazing down, holding a prominent position.

We're not referring to media publicity but the spotlight of customer attention and awareness. It's about looking for opportunities to surprise customers with what you can do for them, if possible beyond their expectations. As it seems like boasting, some people and teams are reluctant to do so. They hold back from deliberately searching for ways of making an impact without focusing attention on the team. But to quote that old phrase, 'If you've got it, flaunt it!'

ACE teams are unwilling to hide their light under a bushel. At the theatre we don't go to hear or see adequate performances. People want outstanding shows, stunning performers. Stars emerge because they strive to shine brightly. Teams must do the same.

It could be taking what you do anyway and making it into something exceptional. In pantomime there's always a moment when pumpkins become carriages and those in rags blossom into princes and princesses. In fact everything changes, and it's called the transformation scene. It should be a moment of magical splendour that touches the child in all of us.

> **Target some customers and think of ten actions you could take to 'show-off' your talents in the area of service.**
> **Now do them!**
>
> *SUGGESTION*

Really that's what team work should be about, making an impact by continually transforming problems into solutions, loss into profit, consumers into customers, enemies into friends, raw materials into product, individuals into teams. Transformation can be a boring old slog or a highly creative, exciting and exploratory experience. It is a choice each team makes.

Peak performance

Another sign of a team's adventurous spirit is its drive to achieve peak performance.

Peak performance feels like flying. Everything works right, first time. Nothing it seems can go wrong. Sports people, actors, dancers, conductors, and players, all tell of performances they have given that felt just perfect. There's an addictive sense of exhilaration and self-fulfilment. Anyone experiencing this wishes fervently it could happen all the time. Of course it cannot, because a peak contrasts with periods when the results may be less exciting.

So peak performance is quite rare. High performance actors, musicians, athletes or business people tend to experience that peak performance feeling several times during their lifetime. They encounter it sufficiently often to recognize it when it's happening, and afterwards to keep reaching for ways to repeat it.

Laurence Olivier once acted a brilliant Othello while on tour in Moscow. Afterwards he locked himself in his dressing room in frustration. When quizzed about why he had retreated after such an achievement, he replied that he knew the performance was exceptional. His frustration was not knowing exactly **how** he had done it!

There are no instant answers, unless you count discipline, dedication and practice. Beyond these, though, there has to be generated a sense of excitement, commitment and raw hunger for peak performance. Though you may expect and welcome it, you cannot merely wish for it.

We're talking therefore about exceptional results. These happen when people and teams are working to such high levels of performance that people, doing their different jobs are totally in tune with everyone else. It is as if some sort of telepathy is present, and in some unknown way perhaps it is.

Few business teams operate at this level of achievement. Instead we hear anodyne clichés such as 'the bottom line', 'It's profit that really counts' or 'Our customers come first'. So what will promote high performance?

It takes team members intense periods of working and playing together. They also need to have a deep respect and trust for each other, before they can regularly expect to achieve results that go beyond just being effective. When teams learn to do this, exceptional results occur. There are legendary performances by great sporting teams – England in the 1966 World Cup Final, Australia winning the *America*'s cup, Europe's first Ryder Cup victory, Australia winning the Rugby World cup, and so on. The same could be said of certain artistic events – memorable for their sublime achievement.

But can we really expect that sort of result in business? Why not? In so many companies there is no spirit of adventure in which these results might flourish. What we know from the performing arts is that peak performance is possible, addictive and does not necessarily takes years to achieve.

The requirements for reaching peak performance are

PREPARE
LET GO
IMPROVISE
USE ENERGY

Let's look at each in detail.

Preparing

At the theatre or cinema you only experience the finished product as a moment when everything comes together – and it looks so easy. You never see the months or even years of preparation.

Peak performance is essentially built on the foundations of careful preparation. The honing of skills, the perfecting of techniques, the refinement of methods all combine eventually and culminate in that precious moment of truly exceptional performance. The three most important actions required for an excellent presentation are rehearse, rehearse and rehearse, and they apply also to a team. Get it right before you ever meet the market place and you can feel free to let go.

Letting go

Letting go is a shift of focus, not just doing more of the same. The power of the team's preparation is that it can afford to look at qualitatively different ways of doing things. This is a time to end all that frenetic activity and do something different.

For example, we worked with a sales team that had spent an enormous amount of time, effort and money learning and practising a sales system. They had discovered how to assess a customer's needs by means of open questions, establish an interest in the product, excite the customer further with the benefits, and, lastly, how to handle any objections from the customer and turn them into possible selling points. They even had a script that allowed them to lead the customer along a path that should inevitably culminate in closing the sale.

However, they weren't getting the results. Something else had to happen. They had to learn to let go. We worked with them on changing their focus, from concentrating on the script and sales procedure to concentrating on something else. That something else was exploring their relationships with the customer. When they were with a customer, in a way, they had to forget about the sales system and the script, and instead rely on their natural instincts as human beings to build the relationship. Then the system could support rather than dominate them.

Teams that cannot let go work ever harder with no real advance towards peak performance. Instead of effortless achievement, there is a grinding struggle. It's much like banging on walls to escape from a room, finding this doesn't work, but simply continuing to bang even more strongly. If only one stops and shifts focus, one might see the door in the wall.

Trying harder doesn't help a singer to reach high notes, for example. According to the singing coach David Krauser, 'Since high notes use the least possible amount of air, they're actually easy to sing. But if you approach them as difficult, they are. Trying hard in fact, never helps – it throws the whole instrument out of balance'.

So for teams letting go means recognizing the right moment to shift focus. It may sound a bit elusive, yet when you are committed to peak performance, there's always a moment for simply trusting in what you have already done.

To use that sales team as an example again, there was a time when its members had put a lot of work into generating new clients. They spent hours, days, weeks on the phone setting up appointments. They reached the stage when it was becoming a way of life. However, they weren't leaving any space for the results to show up. They were so busy carrying on with their struggle to get customers, they didn't realize that they had already built enough of a platform for the response to occur. They now needed to change tack and receive the rewards of their labour.

How does a team recognize the time for letting go? Stage performers would probably say it is when the effort to prepare begins to yield smaller and smaller gains. Business teams might say it is when they must start working smarter, rather than harder.

All that preparation **creates a structure** of certainty, confidence and readiness. Within it, the team can cease trying so hard and simply step into the unknown. It is like when a team has prepared for months to negotiate a major contract, and, having immersed itself in the task, now stops rehearsing and relaxes, trusting that it can deliver. There's a willingness to lose control, which may scare people yet it is what's needed. You cannot control peak performance, only provide the right conditions for it to flourish.

If letting go sounds scary, that's perfectly understandable, since peak performance is both frightening and exciting. No wonder so many teams prefer not to attempt star performance!

Having prepared, the team trusts the process it has set in motion, and allows itself to explore something new in its relationship with its customers – improvising.

Improvising

For years audiences have watched jazz musicians improvise, producing amazing music with apparent ease. Their aliveness is infectious. Actors too have always improvised, and more recently there's been a plethora of theatrical events, radio and television programmes that exploit these talents.

> **SUGGESTION**
>
> It's now performance time.
> It is no good working on last year's accounts to run the finances of the company today. They were useful for setting budgets and projections, but now they need to be stored away for reference. It is time to move on.
> Is the team still concentrated on tasks and practices that, while useful for preparation, are no longer producing any major benefits?
> It's time to stop doing more of the same. Now it's right to let go of certain procedures, routines, expectations and systems. Time to let go of everything, from office files and other clutter to past attitudes and feelings. Create some space for new things to happen by trusting in the work already done.

This is not much different to what happens increasingly in fast-moving, growth-minded companies. They demand similar improvising skills with teams working on problems that reach beyond conventional wisdom. Such work demands speed of thought, sensitivity to others, and trust in one's natural ability to create in the moment. Like the improvising performers, business people need to cultivate quick-wittedness, responsive relationships, acute listening and thrilling creativity. That is why theatre exercises and role plays are so powerful during team training and development.

Using energy

When an ACE team is exploring peak performance, you cannot help noticing that individually and as a group they seem to be buzzing with life. It's different from the purposeless, frenetic busy-ness that so often characterizes organizations. What's special about this kind of buzz is that it occurs when performance energy is focused and channelled. It's what the Japanese are attempting when they start the day in a car factory with some martial arts exercises or Tai Chi.

Our Western tradition is not as repulsed by such tactics as it might seem. In several Japanese factories that have started in Europe the same routines of work-outs, company affirmations or songs have been introduced with great success.

Beginning the day doing press-ups or singing songs is not for every team, and for many it remains alien. Yet people do need help in raising energy levels, especially when they are attempting to achieve peak performance, which is itself demanding. So theatre games, as well as the sort of physical limbering and tuning in exercises mentioned in earlier sections, can be of great use.

Energy is also linked directly to risk. When teams are brave enough to reach for peak performance, it seems to stimulate people and release energy. The presence of energy in a team helps the team to take risks. It's a benign circle.

Risk

> **"I tell them very often. I don't mind mistakes here and there, but I want atmosphere. If you just do a perfect concert, that for me is the worst. In this kind of relationship, you have to be very open towards each other, and when you are open it is easy to get wounded and the natural instinct is to protect oneself. If you take the risk, and you succeed it's incredible. That's what happened in Beethoven's Fifth. It's like a marriage that began to work."**
>
> *Franz Welser-Möst,*
> *Musical Director of the London Philharmonic Orchestra*

Willingness to take risks is the other characteristic of exploring teams that makes an impact. Life itself is risky, but for star performance you go beyond merely living and instead work adventurously. As Porche Chief Executive Peter Schutz once put it, what he sought in those he hired was 'courage. You can't teach them that'.

You know when you're taking a risk – your body tells you. It will always include a rush of adrenalin and physically you will shake, even if only a little. One of the things about taking risks as a team is the scintillating excitement of sharing those feelings with the group.

One of the authors used to appear on a regular live television show. When it was introduced by the announcer and the opening music played, the atmosphere in the studio was electric. People were shivering with excitement, smiling and joking with each other, wishing each other luck and bouncing up and down like small children at a party. It was their way of preparing for the serious business ahead, and added to the enjoyment of the event.

> **"I have a propensity for taking risks. I would rather be in on the ground floor of something chancy than into something safe that's been around for 50 years. "**
>
> Cathleen Black, publisher USA Today

Not everyone handles adrenalin that way. There's a fine line between nervousness and excitement. The advantage of a team is that mutual support can quickly transform nerves into the buzz of excitement and a willingness to take risks.

Of course, in business, risk is usually minimized, and people often talk of taking calculated risks. If that means looking while you leap, staying aware and awake through the process, then we applaud it. If it means covering yourself left, right and centre, then it kills the excitement. It's a delicate balance.

> **"Don't be afraid to take a big step if one is indicated. You can't cross a chasm in two small jumps. "**
>
> David Lloyd George

Thus to explore with a spirit of adventure is not the same as trying to avoid risk altogether, which is what some teams do. Others, though, may be only too keen on taking risks and have to be restrained. Teams in fact are more willing to take risks than individuals.

> **"If you spend your time trying to avoid risk you are unwittingly taking the greatest risk of all. Failure to adapt. "**
>
> Sir John Harvey Jones

Taking just the right amount of risk helps take a team towards peak performance. Each team must judge for itself what is the right amount and learn to distinguish riskiness from recklessness. After all, merely being in business is a huge risk, and it is all around you. We write this book at a time when more businesses are closing down each day than ever

If you're faced with a risky situation get the team to share their feelings about it. Ask

- What's the worst thing that can happen?
- What's the best thing that can happen?

SUGGESTION

Allow the team to experience their feelings about each possibility to the full. Without belittling the members' feelings, be playful with them; encourage people to express their views in creative and fanciful ways. For example, ask everyone to complete sentences such as:

- This situation scares me because . . .
- The situation makes me feel good/excited/happy because . . .

Try having fun play-acting a funeral for the 'death' of the team. Equally, try enjoying the experience of acting out a celebration of the team's success. Having done both, make a conscious choice as a group to focus on success.

before. Most of them will be surprised that it should have happened to them, given how *safe* they have tried to be. Playing safe will not secure safety. There is no escape route that way! Risk either happens to you, or you create it for yourself. An ACE team finds ways to *choose* its risks and learns how to *handle* them.

We started this scene by exploring how a team can use its adventurous spirit to make an impact with Sam Goldwyn's search for the ultimate story. He may have wanted to start with an earthquake, but we feel a volcano might be more appropriate. After all, volcanoes are the result of huge, buried power forcing itself into the world. ACE teams have the power - it's just a question of seeking the right place to erupt!

ACT THREE - Scene 1 "START WITH AN EARTHQUAKE" - Spirit of Adventure

EXPLORING means turning the team...

Curtain up. Light the Lights. We've got nothing to hit. But the heights......

...INSIDE OUT

MAKE AN IMPACT!

KPOW!

Take care of customers and SHOW OFF your service.

Here's your seat. May I clean it for you first?

we expect PEAK PERFORMANCE

PREPARE

LET GO OF OLD BAGGAGE

AND... IMPROVISE!

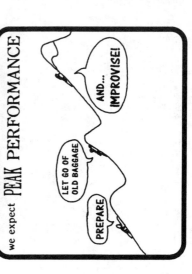

ACE TEAMS TAKE BIGGER RISKS.

SCARY!!

CHOOSE THE PLACE AND RELEASE THE......

POWER

> **"Discovery consists of seeing what everybody has seen and thinking what nobody has thought."**
>
> *Albert Szent-Gyorgi, Hungarian-born US biochemist*

Scene 2 - **'WHO DUNNIT?'**
Growth and Discovery

Growth and Discovery

"There are ill discoverers who think there is no land, when they can see nothing but sea. "

Francis Bacon

Our two directors are leaving the theatre, having watched a long-running thriller.

MANAGING DIRECTOR:	*Great show! Well done. I really enjoyed it. How long's it been running now?*
THEATRE DIRECTOR:	*Over 3 years.*
MANAGING DIRECTOR:	*Well, you'd never believe it. Not at all stale. I don't know how they do it, night after night.*
THEATRE DIRECTOR:	*We've had a few changes of cast, but nevertheless I agree with you, they're a great team. I had a meeting with them earlier today and they were talking about new ideas and interpretations in the play – after performing it for 8 months. They've heard and said the same lines hundreds of times and yet suddenly they'll take on new meaning. It's exciting they're still making discoveries after all this time.*
MANAGING DIRECTOR:	*That's what it should be about, surely? Discovery. Finding out new things all the time, as you go along, and then growing and developing because of it.*
THEATRE DIRECTOR:	*Absolutely. In fact, that's what life is about, for me at any rate. I just want to keep on discovering, learning and developing until I die.*
MANAGING DIRECTOR:	*I've never thought of it like that. In a way, it's a bit like the play we've just watched. It's a mystery, isn't it. You spend all your time as an audience, wondering what's going to happen next, uncovering clues, trying to work it out, getting shocked and surprised en route, and then discovering how it all turns out.*
THEATRE DIRECTOR:	*And it's exactly the same with, say, your team. They're the cast of characters. And the drama and excitement comes from watching the plot unfold.*

| MANAGING DIRECTOR: | *What's going to happen next? What will we learn? How are we doing? What else do we need to do? How will our customers respond? Will we survive? You never know do you, it's a mystery.* |
| THEATRE DIRECTOR: | *A real 'Who Dunnit?'* |

Mysterious goings on

Columbus management: Columbus was like so many managers. He didn't know where he was going, had no idea how to get there, on arrival he didn't know where he was, and anyway someone else had probably got there first.

ACE teams are natural explorers. Because they are adventurous, they are determined to make a difference and an impact on their chosen market. So they're constantly growing and developing, always evolving.

Because they never stand still, no sooner have they mastered something, than they set new goals and move on. Some teams continually recreate themselves. For example, the Apple company has been radically altered several times since its inception, seeing this process as continuous, rather than just an occasional chat.

Other teams reform, break up or even die.

What causes teams to break up or die? Usually when they try to cling to the past, and refuse to adapt. Outside factors are often a catalyst, though seldom the cause; they include takeovers, competitive pressures, reorganization, team members leaving for better opportunities. Occasionally a team simply dies in harness.

Whatever the team chooses to do – evolve, reform, break up or simply die – at the time you never quite know what will happen, how it will turn out. It's a mystery.

The team is faced with unravelling what it's done so far, interpreting what it has discovered, and identifying what else to do. It must decide – either deliberately or by allowing fate to choose – whether to continue, reform or disband. Not so much 'Who Dunnit', as:

- What's happened?
- What have we discovered?
- What else is there to do?
- Will the team live or die?

What's happened?

Like anyone trying to solve a mystery, the team must first understand its present situation – which means knowing where it has got to. Exploring teams continually want to learn where they stand, what are their limits, and whether these have yet been reached. They do so by asking:

- Are we winning?
- Is it working?
- Has it actually happened?
- What have we achieved so far?

This kind of exploration can be difficult, but who said exploring was easy? As high performance teams hack their way through the Amazonian forest of the business world, they know they can easily lose their sense of direction, go round in circles and even fall into a swamp. So they take regular compass bearings. Through 'assessment' ACE teams are continually seeking signs of where they are going, whether and how they are getting there.

The obvious signs are measurable ones, like sales, turnover, profit, staff wastage, share price, and so on. Many of these forms of feedback, though, take too long to reflect the team's performance. When they finally arrive, the whole functioning and situation of the team may have altered. A team needs something more immediate.

It may be more useful for a team to assess 'How have we done?' and for this there are two sources: INTERNAL and EXTERNAL FEEDBACK.

Internal feedback

Internal feedback is what the team can give itself. Many business teams meet regularly, yet the agenda is too often devoted almost entirely to the here and now, the unrelenting day-to-day demands that blot out any scope for true team assessment.

We worked with leading independent mapmaking company Cook Hammond and Kell Ltd, helping it to develop its top team and corporate strategy. At the start of the programme the team found leaving the office for anything other than daily business hard to do. Self-assessment within the team was unknown, and certain problems tended to be brushed under the carpet.

A year later the team had become used to conducting regular assessment sessions in which it explored how it was doing and where it was heading. Company director John Wilders, explains: 'Now we will often stop and say, hey, this isn't working, what else should we be doing? We are now used to taking time off for a couple of days, going away to a hotel and having a look at what is happening and what needs to happen next'.

A similar story took place at the Surrey garden centre we talked about earlier. The management team met regularly – no problem there. But everything was focused on simply keeping the centre running. Virtually no time was devoted to looking at the team's present position, looking ahead to where the team needed to go and the wider company issues.

It took a total restructuring, and the appointment of several new team members, to put assessment back on the agenda. Nor did this process take months or years. Within a week the new team was in place. It was able to handle the day-to-day, while also having the ability to stand back from the daily round of bedding plants and garden furniture to assess what had happened so far and begin developing important new ways for the Centre to grow.

An example of a team having fun with internal feedback is described by Peter Barkworth in *About Acting*:

> I was in Michael Frayn's play *Donkey's Years* at the Globe Theatre. At every performance I gave an eight-minute party in my dressing room. All the actors . . . used to come in, in their dinner jackets and drink Perrier Water (occasionally mildly laced) and talk: we would discuss how the play was going at that performance, and what the audience was like; we would give each other occasional notes and generally chew the fat about plays, actors, directors, critics, authors and impresarios. Occasionally we would play round-robin games: What is the compliment you most like to receive (a) as an actor (b) as a person? Another was: What advice given by other people has most helped you?

Most ACE teams regularly meet to review the group's own impressions of its performance and whether it is being fully stretched. Such explorations can occur on a quick and regular basis, such as weekly breakfast meetings or a team lunch. It's a chance to tune in, as outlined in Act 1, and also to assess questions such as 'How well we are working together?' and 'Is there anything getting in the way of the creative functioning of this group?'

It makes sense to explore these sorts of question, and in a focused, undisturbed environment. Such meetings are best when they occur away from the busy office, in a quiet spot where everyone has time and space to reflect. Among star performers a quarterly assessment meeting of a day or half-day is quite common.

> **"Whether you're an artist, an actor, a writer, in business, or whatever you do, you should have a barometer of what's truthful and what isn't truthful in your work. You have to be able to look at your own work like you're looking at your toughest competitor's work."**
>
> *Dustin Hoffman*

But where will these meetings, which are expensive and time-consuming, actually lead? That's still part of the mystery we talked about earlier. You can't be sure where this process will lead, only that teams wanting to be star performers make time and space for it.

The meetings may start with an exploration of roles and then look at relationships or what results the team now wants. This uncertainty, combined with the personal or intimate nature of the revelations that may occur, can make many teams reluctant to tackle assessment. Some even worry that our team 'won't survive the experience'.

If a team is really that vulnerable, it's unlikely to hold together or be effective for long anyway. But the anxiety is still understandable. Exploring these areas can be risky, and just as a cast of actors needs a good director, sensitive to their needs, so a business team may need help with steering its assessment process. Ideally the team leader should be able to do it. In practice the formal leader is not always the best or most experienced person to handle what may be a tricky process. Occasionally it's sensible to use an outsider who has a good understanding of group processes and communications.

Skilled consultants can reduce the riskiness of team assessment by helping with the more sensitive work, such as exploring relationships. Disintegration of a team under these circumstances is rare. The result is nearly always to strengthen and enliven the team, giving it new energy and a revitalized sense of purpose.

On the few occasions when a team handles its assessment process badly, that still tends to have a positive effect, freeing certain individuals finally to do something about their own lives. What is important is that the team is willing to explore in this way.

For some people this kind of internal feedback is too incestuous and smacks of navel-gazing. It's certainly true that the search for internal feedback can be overdone. There needs to be a healthy balance with external sources.

External feedback

Performing arts teams are directly assessed through external feedback via their audiences. The latter boo, laugh, cheer, cry, stand and applaud, shout out and even throw things. The media give them fast feedback too. At West End premieres, for example, there's a mass exodus before the final curtain call as the critics rush to make their first editions.

Critics are useful, since at their best they are the performers' 'outside eye',

> An interesting and enjoyable way to help a team assess how it is currently working is to ask the members to use symbols or metaphors to describe how they see the team's present functioning. You could even use objects around the room or images. For example, the team might be seen as:
>
> • A kettle: we take a long time to come to the boil, but when we do, we make a great deal of noise about it. We let off steam – sometimes so much steam that we can't see where we're going.
> • A tunnel: we're busy working in the dark for a lot of the time, trying to link two parts of the organization together. People use us without respect for all the hard work we put in. They take us for granted. Perhaps we should close ourselves off for a few days – then they would appreciate us.
> • A gyroscope: we seem to be wobbling precariously on a string and don't always know who or what is holding the ends. We could fall off any time and there'd be no one to pick us up again.

DISSENTING VOICE

" One of the reason's I've never been in analysis is I've always been afraid of what I might find out. "

David Bowie

offering insights that contribute to the team's work or its creative process. Good criticism should be a debate with the practitioner. It should be the same with a business team. The more visible a business team becomes, the more it will be recognized by outsiders, and the more it will attract immediate attention and comment.

The sign of a successful team is its readiness to hear and absorb both positive and critical external feedback. With so much available, particularly from indirect sources such as trade and house journals, business pages and other media, it can be hard to make sense of all the information.

The important requirement is to build a picture from all the sources of feedback available. The team may feel ineffective and lacking energy yet still be constantly referred to as 'dynamic'. Equally, a team may feel it is making a huge and powerful impression, only to be called 'an obscure bunch of inexperienced newcomers'. It tends to be the weight of opinion that is useful, or, putting it slightly different, 'If five people call it a horse – saddle up and ride it!'

DISSENTING VOICE

" You can't believe reviews good or bad. "

Joan Collins

However, true performers soon learn which critics and feedback to trust and which to ignore. It is pointless listening to someone whose values and taste you don't or won't share. In fact their particular negative criticism can act as a valuable endorsement: 'If they don't like it, then it must be right'.

" ... I always think when everybody says something is going to be complete dog, you can be sure it might make some money. "

Leslie Hill, Managing Director of Central Television

There are many indicators from the outside world that will help the team's assessment of itself:

- How many telephone callers, finding their regular contact unavailable, are happy to speak to another member of the team?
- Is the group regularly referred to by the outside world as 'The team from . . .'?
- How open are people about giving the total team feedback about its performance?
- If somebody comes to visit a member of the team at the office, do they say 'Hello' to the other team members?
- If you tell somebody about something that the team did – say, 'We won an enormous new contract' or 'A client has just left us to go elsewhere' – do they seem surprised, or do they treat the news as routine?
- Do you ever get invited out as a team?

An external feedback to our own company team came, for instance, when a respected client took the trouble to ring and say, 'Just thought you should know your last mailing arrived with mistakes in it. We see you as a high quality business and that mailing didn't match our expectations of you'. Galling, but invaluable evidence about our performance! Not long afterwards we hired a new administrator.

Obtaining useful external feedback may require ingenious or even courageous measures. One effective team we heard about wanted to assess how it was doing with customer care. It hired an independent film unit to visit customers and video their responses to pointed questions. Then the team members watched the results and later showed them to everyone who dealt with customers. When the telephone operators, for example, saw actual customers complaining about how long it took to get their calls answered, they started a whole new company effort to improve their performance.

British Airways was also determined to encourage its customers to give their assessment of the service. So they erected video booths in airports. People could make a brief tape explaining what they felt, which gave them a feeling they were actually talking to the chief executive or top team.

Teams need imaginative ways to encourage outside feedback, particularly when embarking on a major project or piece of work. What is required is the equivalent of the preview audience.

Many movie producers and directors preview their films before releasing them. Audiences are invited to attend a showing without knowing anything about the particular film. Mel Brooks, responsible for many box-office hits, sits at the back taking notes during his

> Make a list of all the team's audiences and critics - all the people who might be able to review the team's work. This is your support network. It's a network of people who will, over a period of time, get to know the team's output and can be encouraged to comment on it.
> What ways are the team providing to encourage these potential critics to contribute?

his previews. He observes when people are laughing or yawning, and uses the assessment information to complete a final edit of his film. Many theatre companies these days run the show for a few preview performances to refine it in the light of audience reaction, before officially opening it to the critics.

Business teams need the equivalent, advance information. This happens of course with a new product, which is often tested in the market, but the results are rarely directly relevant to a particular team's performance. By the time market-research companies come into it, the ownership of a product has spread throughout many departments in an organization. It's hard to get direct feedback on the group from such exercises.

So ACE teams look for ways to generate advance assessment information that will help them decide how they are doing.

What have we discovered?

Teamwork is about discovery, unravelling mysteries:

- We did that well, how can we do it again?
- We did that badly, how can we avoid doing it again?

- What have we discovered about our strengths and weaknesses?
- How near are we to becoming an ACE team?

> **" Discovery consists of seeing what everybody has seen and thinking what nobody has thought. "**
>
> *Albert Szent-Gyorgi, Hungarian-born US biochemist*

Exploration does not always take place away from the job. Teams can explore regularly during their weekly or monthly meetings. Just so long as they do it sometime!

How, though, does a team know how close it is to being ACE team? After all, teams vary in their abilities and in different areas. In essence the team question is '**How good, i.e. effective, are we?**'

Many methods for assessment have been developed in recent years. Some, like the Belbin method, concentrate on describing key roles that individuals take within the team. As already suggested, however, despite the undoubted importance of roles, they are only one element that makes an ACE team. Other methods try to highlight blocks the team may be facing, and indicate appropriate ways to remove them. Another way of assessing the team is using the three ACE team dimensions of Aligned, Creative and Exploring to assess the team processes, and thus what aspects of the team may need developing or improving.

By completing a simple questionnaire, either manually or by computer, the team can plot its profile on a chart like the one on the next page.

ACE TEAM DIMENSIONS
Strong on alignment

The team is sure of its core values, has clear leadership, and common objectives. It is highly organized, with clear team roles. There is respect for the individual, with a supportive atmosphere when the group meets. Everyone is fully committed to what the team is trying to achieve.

Strong on creativity

People are always being encouraged to experiment; disagreement is seen as healthy and a way of making things better. Mistakes are tolerated, as well as certain kinds of failure. The team frequently faces really tough deadlines and pressures yet still finds room for sharing strong feelings and emotions. It is fun working together and there is mutual trust. Each person is encouraged to express every aspect of his/her personality.

Strong on exploring

The team occasionally performs brilliantly, as if nothing could go wrong and there always seems to be boundless energy. Team members are usually buzzing with aliveness. Everyone recognizes the benefits of taking risks, and most enjoy taking

The ACE Team Profile

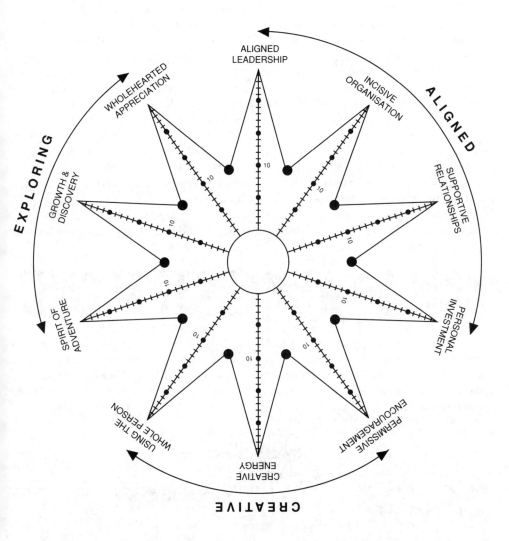

Creating Star Performance In Business

them. The team has a high profile in the organization and gets results. It also regularly assesses its strengths and weaknesses, always seeking new ways to avoid complacency and to enliven itself. Through opposition and challenge the team explores new areas, stretching itself to the limit. It readily acknowledges successes and achievements.

Another approach is for the team to discover what it has learned about the market or the product. What does the team know now that it didn't know before? When Edison was asked about conducting so many unproductive experiments before inventing the light bulb, he replied 'At least I know thousands of ways *not* to make a light bulb!'

When a team is stuck, not sure what to do next, or simply taking time to explore its present situation, it is worth reviewing the accumulated data. This is information about itself, the workings of the organization, networks, the working of the product or service, the efficiency of the company and so on.

How does one make sense of all this data? If we assume that the team is standing back for a moment, conducting an assessment, it can simply explore all the things it has learned and discovered since the last time it conducted such a review. If it's the first time, then the team reviews what it now knows that it didn't know when it started. One of the main strengths of a team is its ability to handle large amounts of data. It can usually quickly decide what are the main learning points, even if it needs help in handling the process.

The next stage in the assessment process is exploring **what else there is to do**. This should stem naturally from the assessment work already completed, using both internal and external feedback. The team may need to awake to new ideas and new possibilities. This is particularly hard when the team has existed a long time, and it may have become complacent and need to ask:

HOW DO WE KEEP IT FRESH?

Complacency is the greatest threat to ACE teams; it drains energy, kills creativity and deters the exploring instinct. The more successful the team, the greater the resistance it may offer to any action that alters either the team or how it's working. The reaction is summed up in the view 'When things seem to be going well, why meddle?' We call this team response the:

MOUSE TRAP SYNDROME

This syndrome applies as much to business as the theatre. Continually refreshing a cast and crew of a long running show is a major challenge. The supreme example is Agatha Christie's *Mousetrap*, now heading toward its half century. The forces of inertia almost guarantee stagnation, prevent creativity and eliminate any exploring instincts.

With the Mousetrap syndrome people get totally bored, and that breeds forgetfulness. We forget that some people are hearing our message or encountering the team and its work for the first time. What may be incredibly familiar to the team is, however, still new or strange to others. So the Mousetrap syndrome can lead a team to make a host of assumptions that ought to be challenged or rethought.

> **" Acting is like tennis. We hit the ball to each other and the audience follows the ball. Now it's your turn, now it's mine. And when it's my turn you must not distract. You must just listen to me. And try to listen to me as though for the first time. Never forget, you do not know what I am going to say, right up to my last syllable. You must not anticipate what I am going to say. "**
>
> *Edith Evans*

Just as an actor needs to remember the audience haven't previously seen the play, so a business team may need to remind itself that EVERY NIGHT IS A FIRST NIGHT. That is, the sales team, the telephone research unit, the management team presenting its vision, may all have repeatedly expressed their ideas over weeks, months, even years. Yet somehow they must still remember that other people may be hearing the message for the first time.

We worked with a team of computer people who had spent 3 tough years developing a new system for a large financial organization. They were about to embark on a series of presentations to let people know how this brilliant new system could support their departments.

Yet the clear message from the team in its presentation was 'We are bored!' They had worked on the project for so long and encountered so many difficulties that instead of conveying 'Here's a great new system to make your life easier' they were really saying 'We've sweated blood over this and we're fed up, but here it is anyway!'

We worked with this team to reanimate their initial enthusiasm for the original project. We encouraged them to put aside their struggle and exhaustion, which were irrelevant to the customers.

Finally, we helped them remember their audience was hearing about this system for the first time – so all jargon and taken-for-granted concepts were banned. The team avoided the Mousetrap syndrome by learning to see it from the audience's fresh point of view.

The best ways of avoiding the Mousetrap syndrome and staying fresh are:

SHAKE UP

NEW INPUT

OPPOSITION &

CHALLENGE

Shake-up

In the theatre recasting once or twice a year helps provide shake-up. In business this is possible through re-forming teams regularly, creating temporary project groups, arranging short-term job swops, and shadowing other people's roles.

Some managers, for instance, swear by certain powerful forms of shake-up. When they acquire a company, become responsible for a department, or even take over a team, they go straight for a dramatic jolt through actions like restructuring, hiring and firing, moving people around and so on. This kind of action is fine as long as it's appropriate, and not used as a panacea for all situations.

Company doctor David James was asked to rescue Dan Air in 1990. He took over on condition he could clear out the entire Board because that's how he often operated. But he needed someone with heavyweight airline experience and didn't recruit them for another seven months. James' shake-up was the wrong medicine and by late 1992 Dan Air was broke and 4500 jobs were lost too.

" The art of governing consists of not allowing men to grow old in their jobs. "

Napoleon Bonaparte

In many permanent teams there is also the continuous danger that people become set in their ways and indeed roles. For instance, when one member of the team is good at producing original ideas or suggestions – the Plant in Meredith Belbin's team classification – it becomes tempting for everyone else to believe that they cannot do the same. An accountant may assume his or her only role is to be an expert on finance, or meetings of the team are always chaired by the same person, so that the rest of the group gradually cease taking any responsibility for functions such as timekeeping, creating agendas, summarizing and so on.

Basically a shake-up comprises measures to attack routine. It is better for the team to explore and discover these itself, than waiting for people outside it to impose their own, perhaps less appropriate, shake-up solutions.

Here are some ideas that have come from a team's brainstorming session around the theme of 'Break it apart and shake it about':

- Change the environment.
- Turn the desks the other way round. Swap places. Swap views. Change secretaries .
- Have a rota of different people to liven up each day.
- Play music.
- Change the work-times. Work all through the night once a week, then have a day off.
- Spend a day in silence (as much as possible).
- Run everywhere.
- Cut all phone calls to under a minute.
- Have a theme for the week.

New input

The bigger the company, the more easily teams seem able to avoid inflicting shake-up on themselves. They so often tend to wait until an outside factor causes it for them, such as an internal reorganization, a new senior manager, a takeover, a market threat, a financial problem and so on.

According to an Ashridge research study in 1989, the main triggers for change in

European and US companies were financial losses (24 per cent), increased competition and loss of market share (23 per cent) and a new chief executive officer (16 per cent). In other words being proactive rather than reactive was quite rare. According to the Ashridge researchers, opportunities or threats that were foreseen only accounted for 23 per cent of changes made in the organizations studied.

Can you wonder that ACE teams and star performance are still quite unusual!

IBM is perhaps the most recent major example of a company that until recently had allowed complacency to permeate its key teams, with a resulting significant loss in market share and serious mistakes in fighting back.

Rather than waiting for outside forces to deliver a shake-up, ACE team will actively invent their own fresh inputs. For example, a team can keep itself fresh by inviting others to join it regularly to inject new information, perspectives and energy. This was the original idea behind non-executive directors. Unfortunately, as research by the PA consultancy organization has shown, too many of these are appointed on the wrong basis and are unable to provide the sort of new input required.

Bourne Leisure is a highly successful company that runs holiday homes and caravan parks. It asked us to look at its sales operation. We asked, 'If it's working successfully, why pay outsiders to investigate?' Robert Seaton, one of the directors, explained it succinctly: 'Maybe we're missing something'. His desire to continue to grow through discovery and have a fresh input put a lie to the old maxim, 'If it ain't broke, don't mess with it'. These days it's more relevant to say, 'If it ain't broke, what will you do if it does?'

Opposition and challenge

Somebody said it couldn't be done,
But he with a chuckle replied
That maybe it couldn't, but he would be one
Who wouldn't say 'no' till he'd tried.
So he buckled right in with the trace of a grin
On his face. If he worried he hid it.
He started to sing as he tackled the thing
That couldn't be done, and he did it.

'You can't do that . . .' must be the single most discredited phrase in the entire English language. Teams, entrepreneurs and companies have so often flown in the face of opposition or disbelief to ultimately triumph that one can almost say

THE OPPOSITE IS TRUE

Some of the most exciting works of art are those where people have done the irreverent, outrageous, unforgivable. The artist Cristo, who wraps buildings or structures such as the Eiffel Tower in material, gets people to look at things in different ways. Performing theatre 'in-the-round' seemed a crazy idea to people who we used to the proscenium arch.

The same goes for business. Examples include McDonalds' Ray Kroc breaking all the rules about how to sell meals and inventing fast food; Apple Computers defying the IBM line of standardization, then stunning everyone in the industry by tying up with its erstwhile rival; Body Shop disdaining the norms of the cosmetic industry; and the introduction of 'just-in-time' production systems against all expert opinion of their workability. Being different can really pay.

❝ We thumbed our noses at rules and procedures. ❞

Perry Rosenthal, Chairman, Polymer Technology, 1987

Going against logic, convention, and traditional practice is hard if you are the first one. It's so much easier when someone else leads the way! Yet ACE teams thrive on challenge, opposition and breaking what others may see as 'the rules'.

DISSENTING VOICES

On the possibility of talking pictures:

❝ Who the hell wants to hear actors talk? ❞

Harry Warner, Founder of Warner Bros Studio

On computers:

❝ There is a world market for about five computers. ❞

Thomas J. Watson of IBM in 1943

To die or not to die?

So far we've assumed the team is alive and wants to stay that way. That's sadly not universally true – some are dead or dying. Watch out for the zombie team, whose spark of life spluttered out long ago, yet it continues regardless. The body functions but it's empty inside.

Zombie teams go through the motions, pretending to be achieving things, but don't. They are the walking dead, and organizations are full of them. Some board meetings are just like that. The directors dutifully meet and practise a ritual. What might have once been a live group is now effectively a dead one. It's just that the corpse refuses to lie down. The best way to avoid this zombie horror is to be an exploring team, able to use and respond to the assessment process. Sometimes, though, it may mean closing the team down.

Some teams function at an incredibly high level of success. Are we really saying one should kill them before they slow down or become less productive? Sometimes that can be the best step. There are many brilliant stage companies, for example, which, despite their success, no longer exist: Belt and Braces, London Contemporary Dance Company, 7:84, Ken Campbell's Roadshow, the Actors Company and many others. A quick death may be better than a long, painful decline.

In business the idea of forming teams quickly, and equally quickly disbanding them to reform different ones, is becoming standard practice in fast-moving, growth-minded companies. This process combats the tendency for teams to turn into committees and become self-perpetuating.

It can be hard to call it a day: it's as if we are calling the individual members failures. Victor Hugo argued, 'Nothing is so powerful as an idea whose time has come', and you could equally say, 'Nothing is so powerless as a team whose time has passed!'

> **" I don't have the same nagging ambition that I had – so I'm glad to take a break. And as a company – we don't have to go on forever. "**
>
> *Michael Pennington,*
> *Joint Artistic Director of the English Shakespeare Company*

There's something healthy about noticing when a job has been done and ending it. We sit down to dinner, finish our meal and place the knife and fork on the plate. If it's been a good meal, we give a sigh of satisfaction. That moment is a moment of completion.

In business, people often prevent that moment from happening. They hold on because they are anxious about facing the insecurity of what next. In terms of a meal, that would suggest continuous eating just to avoid the rest of the day. So it is in many teams – they cling to the past and familiarity.

It may be time to down tools and move on. This is why, in Act One Scene 2 on Incisive Organization, we were advocating dividing work into project chunks that have clearly defined beginnings and endings. At least you then know you have reached some kind of conclusion. That may be when the team needs to disband. Talking of endings, it's time to bring the curtain down on developmental discovery as we move on to

ACT THREE - Scene 2 "WHO DUNNIT?" - Growth and Discovery

The MYSTERY is...
What's going to happen to the team?
Will it....

GROW?

REFORM?

TRANSFORM?

or DIE?

It all depends on what the team has *DISCOVERED.*

How are we doing?

FEEDBACK

The Daily Discoverer
BUSINESS REVIEW

No Turn Unstoned.

The Star Performers ———
at this Year's ——

Keep it *FRESH*

Cheers. Here's to our second anniversary.

It's as if we started yesterday!

NIGHTMARE ON TEAM STREET
"ZOMBIE AND SONS"
The Case of the Walking Dead

I'm sorry, but there's absolutely no sign of life.

Pity. They've been running our sales division for the last 3 years!

TO DIE
OR NOT TO DIE?

ACE
TEAM
R.I.P

Next

> **"When someone does something good, applaud! You will make two people happy."**
>
> *Sam Goldwyn*

Scene 3 - **'APPLAUSE, APPLAUSE'**
Wholehearted Appreciation

Wholehearted Appreciation

" Nothing I know,

Brings on the glow,

Like sweet applause. **"**

From the Musical Applause, Applause

Our two directors are having a celebratory meal in a restaurant.

THEATRE DIRECTOR:	*Well done!*
MANAGING DIRECTOR:	*Thanks, it's been a long haul, but the results are wonderful.*
THEATRE DIRECTOR:	*Good news! I have to say, I think you've done a brilliant job.*
MANAGING DIRECTOR:	*Well, I have a great team.*
THEATRE DIRECTOR:	*But you created them.*
MANAGING DIRECTOR:	*They were good people.*
THEATRE DIRECTOR:	*You chose them.*
MANAGING DIRECTOR:	*They chose themselves really.*
THEATRE DIRECTOR:	*And your leadership was invaluable.*
MANAGING DIRECTOR:	*I honestly think they could have done it without me.*
THEATRE DIRECTOR:	*Oh I give up!*
MANAGING DIRECTOR:	*What?*
THEATRE DIRECTOR:	*Look, you need filling up.*
MANAGING DIRECTOR:	*Oh no, I couldn't possibly drink any more.*
THEATRE DIRECTOR:	*Not your glass. I meant you.*
MANAGING DIRECTOR:	*What d'you mean?*
THEATRE DIRECTOR:	*When stage performers have given their all and the curtain falls, they take a deep breath, stand in front of their audience and hope to receive loud and prolonged applause. They need it. They've given*

everything to the audience, leaving them feeling sort of … empty. Certainly very tender. Now, the audience has watched the show, been nourished by the experience. It's their turn. They want to return the compliment and 'fill up' the performer.

MANAGING DIRECTOR: *Oh, I see what you mean now.*

THEATRE DIRECTOR: *On stage it's usually done by the ritual of applause.*

MANAGING DIRECTOR: *In business too sometimes. Although, generally it's done in a small way, with the everyday 'Thank yous' and 'Well dones' of life. And I have to say, I think I'm rather good at that. I pride myself on my ability to praise people. I'm always acknowledging my team and thanking them for their work – 'filling them up' as you say.*

THEATRE DIRECTOR: *I'm sure you are. However, if you don't mind me saying so, you're lousy at receiving it!*

MANAGING DIRECTOR: *What?*

THEATRE DIRECTOR: *Let me tell you about an experience I had. Early in my career, before I became a director, I was an actor, and I played a leading role in a new play. Afterwards a colleague came up to me and said he thought my performance was wonderful. I did my usual false-modesty routine: 'Oh no, it was a great play, good writing, a fabulous part and a superb cast'. To which my colleague replied, 'Listen, you were wonderful. Nobody may ever say that to you again. Just say "Thank you" and enjoy it while you can!' I learnt my lesson.*

MANAGING DIRECTOR: *I suppose you're right. There's something about letting the acknowledgement touch you, in a way.*

THEATRE DIRECTOR: *Yes. It needs to be received. Or people won't bother giving it.*

MANAGING DIRECTOR: *And then people walk around saying 'Nobody ever appreciates what I do!'*

THEATRE DIRECTOR: *Exactly. That's why performers learn to relish their applause. It nourishes them to continue, encourages them to explore other ways to succeed even more.*

MANAGING DIRECTOR: *True. Well. Thank you. In fact, I think I've done a pretty brilliant job. I've created an ACE team, giving a star performance, in a matter of months. And I deserve some credit for it.*

THEATRE DIRECTOR: *I'll drink to that!*

Achievements deserve appreciation

Congratulations! You've stayed for the final scene of this last act. Thank you for persevering. If we were right there with you, you'd hear a ripple of applause, feel a pat on the back, to acknowledge your achievement. Are we trying to tell you something? Yes, it is:

The theatre world in particular is laughed at for its over-effusive compliments. People think 'Darling, you were absolutely wonderful' is how all actors lavish praise on each other – no matter how terrible the performance has been. Even if the compliments are excessive, however, and occasionally meaningless, they serve a purpose that outsiders may miss.

Applause, appreciation and recognition are a life force – they energize, inspire and renew creative effort. Without them the best performers and their best-conceived ventures falter. When a stage performance has been awful, the 'Darling, you were wonderful' is often merely an expression of fellowship and understanding about what even a poor performance demands.

So how relevant is this life force, which for convenience let's just call applause, to people in business and their teams? We don't think people in business are any different from actors. They probably need it even more, since some of the more obvious ways of showing appreciation and giving recognition, such as actual applause, are quite rare.

In our survey of managers in seven major organizations we asked whether they felt their companies publicly appreciated and rewarded good work. The use of the word 'publicly' was deliberate. Many organizations have a habit of rewarding in discreet, near invisible, ways. Over half the managers surveyed said their employers did not publicly appreciate and reward good work. Only one in four felt their employers did act positively in this way.

In a slightly different question on how they were managed, nearly half (45 per cent) felt they would be more motivated by a different form of management.

> **" I consider my ability to arouse enthusiasm among men the greatest asset that I possess, and the way to develop the best that is in man is by appreciation and encouragement. There is nothing else so kills the ambitions of a man as criticism from his superiors. I never criticise anyone. I believe in giving a man incentive to work. So I am anxious to praise but loath to find fault. If I like anything, I am hearty in my appreciation and lavish in my praise. "**
>
> *Charles Schwab, to whom Andrew Carnegie paid $1 million*
> *to run his steel empire*

So applause is needed as much by business people as it is by actors, though the form it takes may sometimes be different. Psychological research has certainly shown that recognition and appreciation are vital in the development of self-esteem, without which people and teams don't work well.

It's more often termed 'stroking' than applause. People feel so much better when they receive strokes in one form of another. As babies we needed physical stroking to know we were safe and loved. As adults we still need the physical comfort from 'stroking'. However, we also need psychological strokes, which often take the form of compliments, or simply another person really noticing us or what we've done.

Yet managers are often quite uneasy when it comes to giving and receiving applause. Particularly receiving it – they can react quite emotionally.

We see its impact during training and team-building sessions, where we regularly use performance ideas, such as unconditional applause. We encourage it at the end of a presentation and at other points during our workshops, such as creative efforts, whether it's a picture they've drawn or a well-argued idea. It's noticeable how many recipients are visibly moved and uplifted by the experience of receiving fulsome appreciation.

People are hungry for applause in organizations. ACE teams develop a culture where applause in its widest sense of recognition, reward, and appreciation are familiar and expected. Sometimes these occur spontaneously, from the natural exuberance that characterizes so many ACE teams. At other times they occur as setpieces, such as sales or marketing conferences.

Spontaneity versus setpieces

Imagine how the English National Opera or the Royal Shakespeare Company would feel if they performed every night and the audience only clapped once a year! Yet that is what happens in far too many companies. Applause is limited, frequently confined to occasional events such as appraisal time. No wonder many people prefer working for over-demanding leaders who have somehow learned about giving praise when it is due.

No one wants to wait for it once a year, say at an Oscar ceremony. There's clearly a distinction between spontaneous displays of appreciation and such formalized rituals as award ceremonies.

That's not to say that these rituals don't play a vital role. There is a place for the well-orchestrated setpieces of curtain calls and award ceremonies. They can be extremely powerful rituals. When Margot Fonteyn and Rudolf Nureyev danced, the ovations were prolonged, with devoted fans expressing their appreciation. Opera stars like Pavarotti and Kiri Te Kanawa provoke a similar response.

Business has its share of formal rituals, and there's even a reference book on *Awards for Business Excellence* – everything from the Young Businessman of the Year and The Value Improvement Prize, to the Best Delicatessen of the Year. Just as performers have their Oscars, Oliviers and BAFTA awards, so business has its trade awards and companies have their prizes. Some people like these events, others loathe them. However, they provide at least one opportunity for appreciation to be publicly shown.

Management and staff conferences can be highly theatrical events, with great opportunities for ritualistic appreciation. People are brought on stage and publicly thanked for the work they've done, or teams can be picked out and have their work as a group celebrated.

It's more difficult when there is no such formalized structure. In which case, it's down to the team members to explore their own way of thanking each other. It's similar to the problem performers face when working in film or television. Having become used to presenting their work and being immediately praised or chastised for it by the audience, they now have to act in isolation.

With a comedy and a live audience, there is not much difference to a theatre performance. In serious TV drama, though, or in movie-making, there are no audiences on the set. The performer is alone with his or her colleagues. Yet the work is just as stretching and the performer as vulnerable. An actor might be required to perform the most sensitive or heartbreaking scene, with a crew of technicians pointing cameras, boom microphones and lights at them. One of the greatest compliments an actor can receive is when, at the end of a particularly gruelling scene, the rest of the team applaud.

When a new piece of film returns from the laboratory at Industrial Light and Magic, George Lucas' special effects company, no one, regardless of their importance, is allowed to watch the shot alone – it is a group effort.

The team as a whole discovers whether it has succeeded or failed. For a really complicated shot, like the chase through the asteroids from the *Star Wars* trilogy, colleagues from many departments crowd into the viewing room. If the special effect is successful, the entire room breaks into applause.

Their response is spontaneous. That's what makes it so rewarding. In stage performances there are also moments when people instinctively applaud. It might be at a particularly exciting moment, or thrilling effect, or even when something goes wrong and the performers improvise their way out of it. These are unprovoked displays of appreciation.

Spontaneous appreciation happens in business too, but companies, teams and individuals are often not as good at it as they should be. Instead applause is more often considered in terms of financial reward.

Paying someone becomes tantamount to applause, which is why there has been considerable attention on remuneration packages. While these are certainly important, they are insufficient. People seldom see money as their top priority, although they need enough to satisfy their main needs. To perform at their best, they usually need a working atmosphere of support and appreciation, even if it is stressful and highly demanding.

To produce such an environment and make it work properly, it needs the creation of specific moments, other than appraisals or reviews, for appreciation to be expressed. Moments such as weekly get-togethers to review achievements, rehearsing new procedures or project endings. All are opportunities to applaud the team's work.

Thus it makes sense to break work into finite chunks with beginnings and endings. ACE teams know the importance of dividing the big challenges into smaller ones, so that each merits a due ration of applause. People then instinctively look forward to opportunities to celebrate and to shout about successes.

This may seem like encouraging boasting, in which people pat themselves on the back and become even more complacent about their performance. To avoid that, the focus needs to be on exploring how best to enliven the team's performance, including the endings, with suitable applause.

Curtain down

Endings in business are as important as in any stage play or opera, where the audience throws flowers and stamps its feet when a wonderful performance finishes. Business needs the equivalent. ACE teams therefore regularly celebrate endings. These constantly change; it's only important that the team knows an important stage has been reached. It could be the conclusion of a project, an individual achievement, the final phase of a product launch and so on.

> **Build in fixed points during a team's work programme for periods of applause.**
>
> These might come when a specific stage of a major task has been reached, on the achievement of a particular result, or simply when a team member has completed a discrete piece of work.
>
> Look for ways to institutionalize the applause process, so it is built into how the team functions and becomes a way of life.
>
> Ask the members of the team to suggest their own list of endings. Encourage them to take responsibility for seeing these are always celebrated.

But why bother? Surely it's more important to move on quickly to the next challenge facing the team? Not so. People need a chance to savour their successes before rushing on to the next activity. If you have a delicious meal and then immediately try and have another, you are likely to end up with indigestion. It's actually cathartic to celebrate endings – turning points that give people space to share their feelings and thus generate energy for a new beginning. By celebrating, an ACE team is declaring it is ready to move on.

Many managers of course prefer not to move into this territory, preferring any applause to be a rather private affair. But applause is about public recognition. Its whole power to renew and energize stems from a sense that one is being valued, recognized, considered worth while. So the impact is muted if applause is reduced to a quiet word in the corridor or a formal moment such as the annual appraisal – vital though these may be.

ACE teams seem constantly to find moments to celebrate publicly. They share their successes in uninhibited ways with departmental colleagues, customers, suppliers and even occasionally with competitors. We have heard of teams that set up systems of celebration throughout their day. There are sales groups, for instance, which ring a bell each time someone makes a sale by phone, and the whole place glows in the reflected glory of the person's success.

In the orchestra pit of the West End musical *Chess* there was a violinist who led the musicians. His lively spirit kept everyone on their toes, even though they had played the same music many times. If someone played particularly well, then the leader might throw him a sweet. This tiny and absurd gesture meant a great deal to the musicians, and it all happened out of sight of the public, who only saw the drama on stage.

So ACE teams are continually looking for opportunities to appreciate each other's achievement – because they want to. It sounds obvious, yet the point we're making is that people give appreciation not because it will help productivity, or because someone has complained about feeling undervalued. It works because people are genuinely appreciative.

> There are endless creative ways of acknowledging successes. How many can you and your team think of within 10 minutes?
>
> People clapping or cheering is only one, obvious way. How about:
>
> • Opening bottles of bubbly?
> • Party poppers and streamers?
> • A secret sign that only the team knows?
> • Banging a drum?
> • Playing a tape-recording of a crowd cheering wildly?
> • Having a celebratory team song?
> • Marking up a success on a big wall chart?
> • Giving out gold star stickers?
> • Or . . . . ?

Since it makes sense, why does it happen so infrequently? Because problems and pitfalls get in the way and stop it happening regularly.

Problems and pitfalls

You cannot easily simulate genuine applause. If not done in an authentic way, it can be counter-productive. The orchestra leader in our story from the West End musical found his own individualistic style. If somebody else took over the tradition and started dishing out sweets, however, it probably would not work. It needs to come naturally from the person.

Some of the blocks that get in the way of a team using and enjoying applause are:

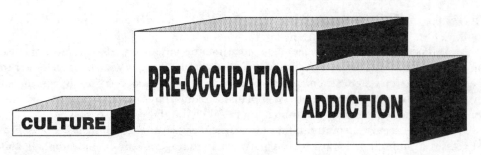

Culture

American audiences are renowned for their enthusiastic standing ovations, readily leaping to their feet to shout and scream approval. Some European audiences, though, are more reserved. It's probably all due to different forms of child-rearing.

Cultural background may prevent some managers too from being able to offer wholehearted appreciation within companies. They feel embarrassed; it may not be in the company tradition and so on. A jaundiced view of how the business world handles the job of giving positive recognition is that 'Some fellows pay a compliment like they expect a receipt'.

Cultural traditions explain why in Britain and some other European nations applause, in its widest sense, can be hard to encourage. It smacks of going over the top, of showing emotion and being over-personal. Or people think they will appear false, and that can certainly happen.

DISSENTING VOICE

" Do not trust the cheering, for those very persons would shout as much if you were going to be hanged. "

Oliver Cromwell

For a team leader or the group as a whole, giving applause can feel at first rather strange, maybe embarrassing. However, it gets easier with practice. A useful starting point is to 'Catch them doing something right'. It is better to look around for what *is* working rather than what isn't.

Expressing how much you value someone or their particular contribution helps the effective growth and development of the team. Psychological research on behaviour modification has also shown the importance of carefully targeted reward and acknowledgement. It is not just another version of the stick and carrot principle.

Behavioural modification research confirms that encouraging even tiny amounts of a desired form of behaviour makes more of it happen. This is called reinforcement. By looking for signs that you can reinforce, you influence the speed and rate of behavioural change.

This is similar to how passionate gardeners work. Caring gardeners don't waste energy cursing and humiliating their plants. You are unlikely to hear shouts of 'Call that a shoot? What a pathetic display!' Instead they lovingly water them. If they talk to them at all, it's more likely to be with gentle encouragement.

Much the same applies in teams at the individual and group level. To perform at its best, the team needs regular reinforcement, the relevant form of applause to show it is moving in the right direction. ACE teams and their leaders constantly look for signs they are moving in the right direction and then reinforce them. Far too many managers, though, seem happier picking on faults than giving a pat on the back.

We are not of course arguing for applause, right or wrong. There's no sense in meaningless applause for its own sake. Saying everything is wonderful when it isn't can be damaging, and people won't trust you. Applause has to be authentic.

Few business teams, however, have failed because people in them have been over-praised. More fail through lack of it. In our work with developing teams the hardest job is persuading people to value applause in its widest sense.

> Try discovering the last time when every single member of the team really felt the applause .
> Ask each member to tell the team:
>
> • When I felt really rewarded working with you.
> • When I felt my contribution was not fully recognized.
>
> Use the results to clarify whether and how the team could improve its feedback to the members about their individual contribution to success.

"He who praises everybody praises nobody."

Dr Johnson

Preoccupation

There are always plenty of opportunities in team work for applause. But the better the team, the busier it becomes, and the less space it may make for celebrations, recognitions, rewards and appreciation. With a hard-driving team leader, it is all too common to lose sight of the nurturing need for applause. The commonest excuse for not giving people and teams their rightful acclaim is 'I'm too busy!' This really hides what is actually happening. Usually the more truthful answer is, 'I didn't think about it. My attention was elsewhere'.

"Once in a century a man may be ruined or made insufferable by praise. But surely once in a minute something generous dies for want of it."

John Masefield

In too many organizations applause is not a priority. Of course there are always more burning issues to be dealt with. All managers are under huge pressures to get results. But ACE teams focus on their process as much as on the results. What is the point of achieving successful results if the team loses its heart on the way? Relationships will be so poor that there will be little fun in the achievement. It takes so little time to applaud your colleagues. It merely needs the decision to pay attention to it, constantly looking for ways to do it, excuses to do it, and people who deserve it.

> **" When someone does something good, applaud! You will make two people happy. "**

Sam Goldwyn

Addiction

Applause can become addictive, and that too can become a block to making the best use of it. The team may go through an exciting period when everything is going well and there is plenty to acknowledge. People give and receive applause all over the place. Then difficulties arise and people begin to hold back.

Once people start holding back, withdrawal symptoms set in. Where is all the familiar, delicious applause? Team members mope around, feeling unloved and abandoned. So like all dangerously addictive drugs, applause needs to be administered prudently. Used with care, you might even say love, it can be transforming.

Giving and receiving applause

Some ground rules for how ACE teams use applause in its widest sense are:

- Find a genuine reason for giving it.
- Public applause is better than private applause.
- Give it unconditionally, not in a half-hearted way.
- Offer it regularly, not sporadically.
- Applaud effort and courage – not just success.
- Celebrate endings.
- Make applause specific and detailed.

Avoid the all-purpose 'Well done'. What was it that specifically deserved recognition?

If a team or its members is to be praised, let it be generous and open. Typical backhanders include:

- What you have done is great; pity it took so long.
- You're one of the best, make sure you damn well stay that way.
- Terrific result, never thought you had it in you.
- This has been done really well, except for . . .
- There's no denying you've done well this time.
- Great work. Who helped you?
- When you're famous, I'll tell them I knew you when you were nothing!

It can be as hard for some people to receive applause, such as positive feedback, as it is for others to give it. Many of us have developed elaborate mechanisms for avoiding or deflecting praise. Some people can become incredibly embarrassed, particularly if they were chastised for boasting or showing off when they were young. However, as adults, we need to receive our colleagues' appreciation of us if we are to develop strong relationships.

" I deserve this. "

Shirley Maclaine, accepting an Oscar

In many of our developmental programmes we ask teams to acknowledge specific qualities in each team member. We spend plenty of time getting the person ready to receive it. One at a time, each member of the team sits in what we designate the 'magic' chair. This chair miraculously robs them of any ability to speak. They can only breathe and listen.

In this state they really hear what is being said to them. Some people find it extremely difficult to receive the compliments and are desperate to 'talk away' the experience. However, they are invariably moved and make such comments as 'I never knew you felt like that about me' or 'I didn't realize I was valued so much by you'.

Does this sort of thing though have much direct relevance to the average hard-working business team? Well, take, for example, the group of senior departmental heads on which we used the above exercise. The engineer was in the 'magic' chair. The company had been facing many technical problems recently and he was continually being called to sort things out. Since all he had regularly heard from his colleagues were complaints, it was hard for him to realize that while they were critical of the problems, they also fully appreciated him and his determination to solve them. He sat silent, listening to his fellow team members, and received some fulsome and heartfelt thanks from the group. He was totally shocked. He had never considered that they valued his work. It was an absolute turning point for the team.

Coping with stardom

" The price of cauliflowers has gone up. People think you have a lot of money and see you coming. "

Sir John Harvey Jones on celebrity

ACE teams that achieve star performance face one welcome problem that less successful ones might love to have, namely, how to deal with success, and the high profile that goes with it.

The price of success is nearly always pressure to do even better next time. Many successful writers and performers, having arrived in the bright circle of fame, feel the weight of responsibilities to their fans, agents, producers, publishers, colleagues, and many more. It can be a daunting prospect; hence the importance of good support both within and beyond the team. It's back to relationships again.

Some teams never achieve star performance through fear of success rather than failure.

It holds them back. Unconsciously they may sabotage themselves because of a suppressed wish to **avoid** triumph; for then they could no longer plead poverty, play 'hard-done-by', or offer endless excuses – common among some teams. On the contrary, now people would be looking to them as leaders in their field, path-finders and role-models. Staying 'average' is so much more comfortable.

Once a team is winning public applause, all the qualities about relationships described in earlier scenes come into their own. For example, there is always a danger that certain team members will receive more attention than others, which can put a strain on the ensemble nature of the group. When that happens, the answer is to talk openly about feelings and try to spread the focus around, for example taking turns at doing interviews, speaking at conferences, and meeting internal and external customers. In fact once a team is is successful, all the work done to get the team aligned in the first place has to take place again.

Spend some time as a team imagining what it would be like to be a high-profile success:

(SUGGESTION)

• Role-play interviews.
• Write articles about yourselves.
• List all the demands on you if you were stars in your industry.

Then choose whether you really want it or not.
What are the negative aspects to it? How would you as a team handle them?

> ## " Now when I bore people at a party, they think it's their fault. "
>
> *Henry Kissinger*

Stage performers know they cannot rest on past laurels. You're only as good as your last performance. Each new project demands a new commitment and a new level of energy. It is just the same for the star performing ACE business team.

And so we lower the curtain on all three acts of this epic drama. We hope you've enjoyed it and have found it useful. If you are excited and challenged to achieve star performance, we are delighted, and send you our good wishes.

Whatever your experiences, we'd like to hear about them. It will enable us to keep developing our own work. We are quite prepared to handle the ensuing fame!

ACT THREE - Scene 3 "APPLAUSE, APPLAUSE." - Wholehearted Appreciation

RESERVE can create .....

We've just made an amazing, stunning major mega-breakthrough

Oh. Fine.

a team of RESERVES.

HANDLING

FAME

Thanks

Autographs - this way

Find times to celebrate.....

THE END

begin the APPLAUSE!

ENCOURAGEMENT.

Come on my little beauties. Grow big and strong. That's right. That's the way. Here's a little drink for you...

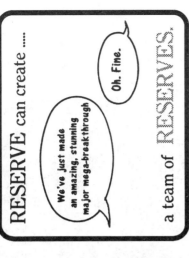

Brilliant.
A Hit.
Hooray
Encore
Marvellous
A Triumph
Incredible
Fantastic
Well done
Bravo

GIVING AND RECEIVING

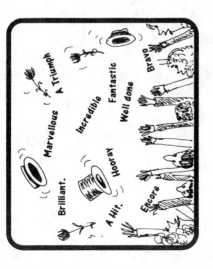

It's hard to acknowledge a moving target.

Must dash.

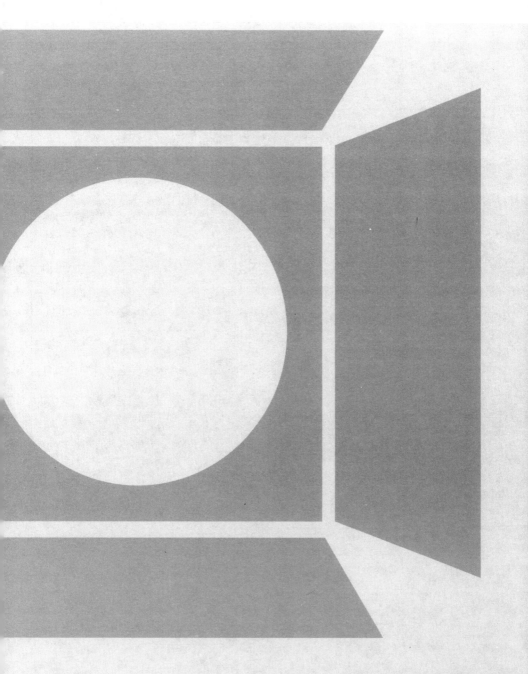

EPILOGUE – 'AUTHOR, AUTHOR!'

EPILOGUE – 'AUTHOR, AUTHOR!'

As the curtain falls on *ACE Teams* and the audience applauds, there are cries of 'Bravo' and 'Encore', and of course calls for 'Author, Author'. Not being ones to miss an opportunity to give the public what they want, the two authors hold a hurried conference:

AUTHOR 1:	*That's it, then.*
AUTHOR 2:	*Yes, end of the whole thing.*
AUTHOR 1:	*We've done it, and they like it.*
AUTHOR 2:	*It was our best shot, we couldn't have done any more.*
AUTHOR 1:	*Umm . . . well . . .*
AUTHOR 2:	*Now what, for heavens sake!*
AUTHOR 1:	*It's struck me we've been explaining how ACE teams always explore ways of going one better and being outstanding. So what about us?*
AUTHOR 2:	*You mean, show 'em we're an ACE team too?*
AUTHOR 1:	*Not quite, they've just sat through the whole show. I mean how do we give even better value?*
AUTHOR 2:	*Deliver the unexpected, superlative service to the customer?*
AUTHOR 1:	*Exactly, so how about an encore?*
AUTHOR 2:	*A reprise!*
AUTHOR 1:	*Yes, I like it.*
BOTH:	*So let's go!*

ALIGNED LEADERSHIP is . . .

inspired direction, enrolling people to produce
outstanding results

WHAT IS IT ?

Team direction which fires people's imagination, enrols them
in a common vision and set of values, and encourages
everyone, to fully contribute in their own special way to the
group's aims.

HOW DO WE RECOGNIZE IT ?

People show commitment to, and ability to communicate, the
team's main purpose or vision.
Everyone subscribes to some common values, which also
support the broader vision.
Practical solutions are constantly found for converting vision
and values into exceptional performance.
There is clarity of leadership.
Leadership is conducted within definite time boundaries
during which people give their loyalty.

WHAT RESULTS COME FROM ALIGNED LEADERSHIP ?

People fully express themselves and contribute their unique
talents while still feeling part of a tightly knit group.
No time is wasted on leadership disputes.
Team members build effective relationships with each other
and outsiders as a way of achieving results.
Ideals are converted into realistic programmes of action,
which arc implemented, usually with great success.
What really matters is constantly discussed inside and outside
the team.
The team becomes ready to tackle other important issues that
will help it produce exceptional results.

ALIGNED LEADERSHIP

INCISIVE ORGANIZATION is . . .

commitment by the right people to clear objectives,
firm deadlines and overcoming obstacles

WHAT IS IT ?

A way of arranging people and tasks so they are absolutely clear about what they are doing and are closely aligned on values, purpose, commitment and the importance of creative contribution.

HOW DO WE RECOGNIZE IT ?

People are sure of the team's aims and more detailed tasks.
Regular efforts identify obstacles and appropriate action.
There are firm time scales, which are generally accepted as immutable.
Important aims are constantly broken into smaller chunks with their own deadlines for action.
Team members say much the same thing about the team's values, its purpose and their own commitment to it.
All team members accept the importance of creative contribution to achieving the team's aims.

WHAT RESULTS COME FROM INCISIVE ORGANIZATION ?

The right people combine into a powerful force for achievement.
People's time is focused on relevant actions with few distractions.
Obstacles to progress are constantly overcome.
People know what they have to do to succeed.
Things are done on time.
The team tackles the wider issues of alignment, creativity and exploration.

SUPPORTIVE RELATIONSHIPS ...

willingness to care, share and show mutual respect

WHAT IS IT ?

The positive behaviour of team members towards each other,
such as how they talk and listen to one another.
Being prepared to care, help, listen or simply talk together
about issues that matter.

HOW DO WE RECOGNIZE IT ?

There is openness, honesty and trust between team members.
Team members seem to 'tune in' to each other's needs,
reading the often hidden messages that may need a response
of some kind.
There is a mutual willingness to discuss feelings.
People's differences are respected and valued.
People share ideas, do not hoard information and are willing
to pool ideas for mutual benefit.
Traditional barriers or hierarchy or status are not allowed to
obstruct good team communications.
People spontaneously help each other without having to be
asked.

WHAT RESULTS COME FROM SUPPORTIVE RELATIONSHIPS ?

People become more effective and energetic at what they do.
The building of relationships strengthens the whole team's
effectiveness.
Resolves blocks to action and shows how to get more done.
Enhances willingness to take risks, be creative and handle
pressures.
Joint working, good communications and problem-solving.

PERSONAL INVESTMENT is . . .

full commitment to success

WHAT IS IT ?

The link people make between their own desires and achieving success with other people.
Deep individual involvement arising from making a personal commitment.
Exhilaration from being totally absorbed by something.
Putting personal energy behind one's passion.

HOW DO WE RECOGNIZE IT ?

People act as if the group's success matters personally to them.
Individuals talk about and treat the group's aims as their own.
People appear to gain great satisfaction from what they are doing.
Team members work at building the team's reputation as a way of enhancing their own.
People are excited by the opportunity to do things well.
No job seems too small for some team members, if it enhances the team's chances of success.
Team members may push for public recognition for what they and the team are doing.
There is a constant push to be in on the ground floor of new opportunities.

WHAT RESULTS COME FROM PERSONAL INVESTMENT ?

People behave as if it's up to them to create success.
Individuals will often willingly subordinate their personal ambitions to those of the group.
People work and contribute often beyond the call of duty.
Teams become more aligned on the key issues facing them and how to achieve outstanding results.
There is considerable collective energy and drive to be outstanding.

PERMISSIVE ENCOURAGEMENT is . . .

promoting experiments, valuing disagreements and tolerating certain failures

WHAT IS IT ?

A team climate that starts with 'yes' to initial ideas and suggestions.
Experiments are a way of life and disagreement is used creatively.
Failures are used to learn from, rather than to blame people.

HOW DO WE RECOGNIZE IT ?

Routine, cynicism and negativity seldom prevail.
Hierarchies are not allowed to obstruct ideas, prevent people trying out things, or stop differences from surfacing.
There are always plenty of ideas around and many are being tried.
Disagreements are used to promote progress, differences are valued.
'Yes but . . .' is seldom heard.
People build on each other's suggestions and contributions.
People really listen to each other.

WHAT RESULTS COME FROM PERMISSIVE ENCOURAGEMENT ?

People learn fast about avoiding or minimizing the recurrence of mistakes.
People are constantly trying new things.
People respond to failure by picking themselves up and having another go.
Team members readily offer ideas and suggestions and are willing to say when they disagree.
All team members take responsibility for encouraging the group's creative potential.

CREATIVE ENERGY is . . .

the intensive struggle for star performance

WHAT IS IT ?

It's the exceptional effort to 'go for gold'; the creative team strives to go beyond mediocrity, past competence, on to star performance. The struggle includes play and fun as well as pain and struggle. Teams must learn to handle these extremes of up and down through various means.

HOW DO WE RECOGNIZE IT ?

By seeing teams having periods of great intensity of work.
By observing teams creating opportunities for play and fun.
By watching teams experience inevitable pain and struggle with low productivity and even low morale.
By seeing sudden upsurges of creative team work in which at times absolutely everything seems to go well and all obstacles are pushed aside.

WHAT RESULTS COME FROM CREATIVE ENERGY ?

People and teams bristle with ideas and new ways of working.
Important aims begin to be, or actually are, achieved.
People feel more closely bound together and productive.
There is a willingness to rock the boat and challenge cosy assumptions and old ways of working.
Teams energize and inspire others around them.

USING THE WHOLE PERSON is . . .

fully stretching people

WHAT IS IT ?

When teams use every part of each person – their physicality, intellect, emotions, intuition and even their sexuality – in a balanced, healthy way.

HOW DO WE RECOGNIZE IT ?

People in teams are able to use their bodies as well as their minds to express themselves and to remain healthy.
The intellect of team members is fully stimulated.
Team members are excited and engaged in their work and unafraid to express their feelings and strong emotions.
There are regular opportunities for people to 'blow off steam'.
Sexual differences are acknowledged and contribute to the team's well-being.

WHAT RESULTS COME FROM USING THE WHOLE PERSON ?

Teams use all their human resources not merely one aspect.
Being fully used as a person, each team member is motivated and more alive and thus willing to contribute and take responsibility.
Teams are resilient in the face of hard or stressful situations.
People express themselves and are creative because they feel able to use all of themselves .

SPIRIT OF ADVENTURE is . . .

going beyond team boundaries to make a stunning impact

WHAT IS IT ?

When the team goes outside its own confines to make a significant impact and achieve peak performance. The team and its individuals are also able to take risks and avoid always playing safe.

HOW DO WE RECOGNIZE IT ?

The team breaks the mould and finds its own unique style.
People are willing to make a difference outside the team.
The team builds outside relationships, shares its values widely and builds a high profile.
People's energy is focused and channelled.
The team has a great many balls in the air.
Their is deep respect and trust among team members.
The team is clearly accountable for its work.

WHAT RESULTS COME FROM THE SPIRIT OF ADVENTURE ?

Every opportunity to show how superlative it can be is used by the team.
People are always exploring ways to 'surprise' the team's stakeholders and exceed expectations .
Problems are transformed into solutions, loss into profit and consumers into customers, etc.
There are peak moments when everything works superbly, as if absolutely nothing can go wrong.

GROWTH & DISCOVERY is . . .

*learning from performance and deciding what more is
needed for success*

WHAT IS G&D ?

The process by which a team continually assesses itself, its
performance, and what it must do next to be outstanding.

HOW DO WE RECOGNIZE G&D ?

There is regular feedback to the team, from within and from
sources such as other departments, clients, suppliers, etc.
Teams take time to explore how they are working together
and what might be getting in the way of being creative.
Outside assistance is sometimes used to help focus on a
group's total effectiveness.
The team keeps exploring whether as a whole, and as
individuals, everyone is fully stretched.
Shake-up, new input, opposition and challenge keep the team
fresh.

WHAT RESULTS COME FROM GROWTH & DISCOVERY?

The benefits vary in each team as it constantly takes a fresh
look at issues such as relationships, roles, effectiveness and
how to be more creative and proactive.
The team is more willing to absorb and use positive and
negative feedback from a variety of direct and indirect
sources.
The team stays fresh even when performing the same activity
many times, and avoids stagnation or boredom.

WHOLEHEARTED APPRECIATION is . . .

recognition, reward and acknowledgement, given honestly

WHAT IS IT ?

The recognition, reward and stroking that people in organizations should have, regularly. Sometimes given in a formal way, it is better when naturally spontaneous from the heart, and honest. When people constantly seek opportunities to celebrate success.

HOW DO WE RECOGNIZE IT ?

By making appreciation specific and giving it publicly.
By creating many opportunities for giving recognition and publicly celebrating success.
By having fixed endings to work activity, which are celebrated.
By everyone in a team taking responsibility to give recognition.
By having celebrations that are fun and uninhibited.
Desired behaviour is positively reinforced through appreciation.
Effort and courage are rewarded, not just success.

WHAT RESULTS COME FROM WHOLEHEARTED APPRECIATION ?

Teams and individuals feel valued and therefore more committed to achieving exceptional results.
Pride in achievement and knowledge that success will not go unmarked.
People cope better with setbacks and difficulties because their struggles are acknowledged.
Ability to handle stress and ambitious targets.
Teams and individuals go that extra mile and hunger to do even better.
Team members' self-esteem is high.

STAGE NOTES

This production was made possible with the help of our dedicated stage crew, none of whom can be held responsible for our mistakes. Our special thanks go to: Mary Allen; Martin Cochrane; Dan Fauci; Suzanne Wilson Higgins; Carol Leader; Gillian Leigh; David Mulvey; Michaela Justice; and Allen Shoer; our Associates, past and present; Maynard Leigh Associates' clients and others who kindly gave permission to use their names and case studies.

The authors

After several years on the Business Section of *The Observer* and as senior manager in the public services, Andrew Leigh set up his own consultancy, in partnership with Michael Maynard. He advises on organizational change, team-building, communications and HRD programmes. Author of several books on management, he is also a Fellow of the Institute of Personnel Management.

Michael Maynard, having been a successful actor for 18 years, now leads business and management workshops across the UK and Europe, specializing in creativity, self-expression and communication skills. He leads the acclaimed 'Mastery' course at the Actors Institute in the City of London. A pioneer of theatre techniques in education and subsequently in business, he has written for radio, TV and created many industrial and audio-visual presentation.

Michael Maynard and Andrew Leigh are partners in Maynard Leigh Associates, the development and consultancy service, whose clients include many major corporations.

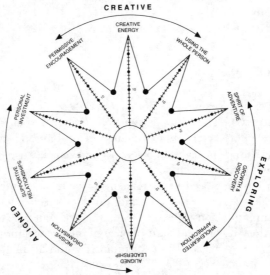